Dedication

I dedicate this book to my Mother and Father.

First Published in 2008
Actikarate
55 Shortmead Street,
Biggleswade, Beds
SG18 0AT

Defending Against Attack "The Shotokan Way"'
1st Edition first published In Great Britain in 2008
by Frank Nezhadpournia

The views and ideas expressed in this book are solely those of
the author and the people with whom he has approached.
Please bear in mind that laws change, and this does not sub-
stitute the readers need to keep abreast of and/or changes in
the law.

This Book is a work of non-fiction. Unless otherwise noted, the
author and publisher make no explicit guarantees as to the accuracy of the information contained in this book.

ISBN 978-0955727-405
Printed and Bound in Great Britain
by Palladian Press Ltd
Distributed by Gazelle Book Services Ltd

Reverse Roundhouse Kick
Ushiro Mawashi Geri

Contents

Contents

Contents

Side Thrust Kick Head Level
Yoko Geri Kekomi Jōdan

Acknowledgements

Azadeh, Farhad, Farima, and baby Scarlet, Riccardo, Natalie De-Vernon, Sue Teale, Erika Jenkins, Nick Cullen, Joachim Gruppe, Jane North, Gina, Ayse, Sylvia at Dartford and Gravesham Women's Aid and Cathy. My lost but not forgotten friend, Paul Wilson for introducing me to Karate!

For keeping me motivated:
To my growing tigers! (My students) Isabelle, Ella, Heather, Jo, Hannah, Maddie, Caroline, Emily, Chenisse, Maggie, Holly, Ellie, Sarah, Jasmine, Emma, Jenny, Chloe, Jack, Natasha, Ethan, Molly, Olivia, Daisy-Mei, Mel, Connie, Elsa, Abigail, Maxine, Holly, Charlie, Tamzin, Liam, Georgina, Amelia, Sophie, Kara, Neve, Caitlin, Julia, Georgia, Jacob, Charlotte, Remy, Cameron, Max, Oliver, Stefan, Benjamin, Joshua, Rhys, John, Alex, Aaron, Edward, Sam, Alyss, Alice, the two James', the two Elliotts', Megan, Angus, Gabrielle, Luke, Jeeven. Georgia, Rosalie, Jack, Ashton, Samuel, Ivan, Ryan, George, Rebecca, Frank, Leonardo, Rosie, Lucas, Malaika, Jade, Ethan, Nathan, Lisa, Matthew, Caitlin, Tilly, Matilda, Scott, Lewis.

All UK Staff working to reduce violence against persons: Ealing, Cambridge, Brixton, Handsworth, Clapham, Harrow, Colchester, Dartford & Gravesham, Milton Keynes, Thurrock, Kent, Brighton, Boston, Leicester, Grimsby, Westminster, Bedford, Hampstead, Greenwich, Hammersmith, Shepherds Bush, East Berkshire, Lincoln, Harlow, Haringey, Luton, Milton Keynes and Loughborough.

The following organisations supporting karate and & its merits: Milton Keynes Lighthouse, Domestic Violence Units, Asha Projects, Connexions, Reaching Out, Milton Keynes Council, Bedford Borough Council Solas Anois, Eaves Housing, Simon Burley (UK Guardian Angels), Stuart King, (Sports Development), Alison Slatcher, (Bedford Development Agency), Jason Foster (Bedford Borough Council), Ahura Kalali, Dirk Zimmerman Berlin Germany, and Fernando "Bloom" Zanna.

Acknowledgements

Fitness First. Kerman Shōtōkan Karate Club, Close to Home, Milton Keynes Youth Service, Outreach Project and Milton Keynes Council. Berlin JKA Group. Mary O'Brien for the Thursday afternoon chats, Mr & Mrs Keeley for supporting my efforts at Carlton! Thank you for your hospitality!

The senior karate practitioners for their on-going interest in my welfare:

Sensei Mike Batten 5th Dan
Sensei Joachim Gruppe 5th Dan
Sensei Robin Packman 3rd Dan

To the schools

To the all of the Head teachers and staff for supporting Karate as an 'After School Activity': Mrs Cantwell (retired), Mrs Sue Birch, Mrs Bell, Mrs Augustine, Mrs Curry, Mrs Johnson-Clarke, Mrs Readyhough. The school secretary's for coordinating activities which were ever changing! Thank you Deborah, Leslie and Corinne, for keeping me organised.

Andrew Grimshaw (Housemaster Bedford School)

Ross Thomson, for his section on Body Language. His observation and love for animals is amazing! The models available on such short notice: Arya Kalali, Daniella Martignetti, Mark Lawn on his brilliant section; Warming up and stretching. Becky James thanks for your support and patience!

Bradley Bruce (juggling rugby with karate, "How do you do it?")
Tom Whalley
Mathias
Mark Slade a true karate practitioner - always striving to learn more and do better!

Foreword

After meeting Frank at the Mathiesen Youth Centre, in Milton Keynes a number of years ago and observing him deliver one of his self-defence sessions to a group of adults, I was really impressed. I decided to have a conversation with him and find out a little bit more about exactly what his work entailed.

After further discussions with him, I was keen to book him in, to teach his self-defence skills to a group of young people that we were supporting on a project called **'Reaching Out'**. Reaching Out is a motivational project that aims to support young people of 16-19 years of age who are not in education employment or training, helping them gain the skills that will motivate them back into the above sectors.

Throughout the 6 week project, the young people develop a broad range of new skills that will help them in life. Frank's sessions really help raise the student's awareness of risks and dangers. The sessions teach how to avoid violence, confrontation and aggressive situations and guide them in developing new skills in effectively managing their own feelings of anger or aggression whilst also channelling these feelings in a more positive direction. Developing self-control and to **'think then react'**.

Frank has been highly successful in supporting a broad range of young people, from different backgrounds and cultures who have presented us with a number of different issues, some who have been a real challenge.

He has always remained calm and highly professional at all times and has gained a great deal of respect and admiration from the young people on the project.

Foreword

He has taught them a range of skills that will have a positive impact on these students for the rest of their lives.

Natalie De Vernon
Close to Home Project Worker
Milton Keynes Youth Service
Milton Keynes Council
15TH October 2007

Telephone: 07946 814892
Email: Natalie.Devernon@milton-keynes.gov.uk

Some Facts!

Violent crime rose on average by 11% in The EU and 20% in England & Wales
Home Office Statistical Bulletin 6/01, May 2001

Some 280 children were expelled from school for assaulting adults, with a further 336 explosions for attacking other children.

A total of 4000 children were suspended for attacking adults and this number rockets to 12,800 for attacks on other pupils.

Most of these were boys and the most common age for attacks was between 13-14 years of age.

The most common offence was persistent disruptive behaviour

Official figures say the majority of exclusions are boys, but the study claims more girls are excluding themselves by not turning up to school if they are having problems, meaning the numbers are not added to statistics.

ChildLine research reveals the worrying state of young people's mental health. One in six calls (1,009) to ChildLine last year concerning mental health came from girls who talked about suicide

For 2004/05, 10% of respondents said that they felt 'very unsafe' walking alone in their area after dark and a further 20% felt 'a bit unsafe'
Worry about crime in England & Wales.
Findings from 2003/04 and 2004/05 British Crime Surveys

A Message To The Reader

"This is a manual teaching students **Basic Shōtōkan Karate** from white belt up to Purple White grade. It is to be used in conjunction with weekly training.

Teaching the categories of **Kihon**, **Kumite** and **Kata.**

I would really like to continue the theme of self defence as in the first book, helping reduce *'Attack Chances'* by understanding attack psychology and the different forms they take. Giving my own personal experiences and those of people I have come in contact with. This is real application! (Bunkai)

If your intention is to learn Karate for merely an achievement of a rank than there are other books on the subject. Karate is a martial art and a system of self defence. It is complicated and becomes intense with grade.

Giving the practitioner confidence, increased self esteem and parents the assurance that there child is more *street aware* and stands a better chance of avoiding attack compared to the person with no training!

It also requires commitment, hard effort and dedication. So we will lose some students along the way. However what they learn they take with them! I hope you enjoy it!

Preface

Frank was born in Ahwaz, Iran to the 'Bakhtiari', (a very old and traditional race of Persians) and moved to the UK at the age 5, where he started his training in Bedfordshire, after a friend suggested they attend a class together. A friend who would later lose his life in a car crash. This class had a profound effect and he has been training ever since.

A traditional martial artist, he was awarded his Black belt after three and half years of hard training. Teaching in sports centres throughout the UK, Middle East and Europe. Affiliated to the **JKA (Japanese Karate Association)** and Chief Instructor to his own association coaching students of all ages. (**ACTIKARATE SHŌTŌKAN KARATE**)

Frank has been very fortunate to have been examined by some of the finest British, Japanese and Iranian instructors in the world learning and absorbing delivery styles in the process. Which he extends in his teaching, keeping as close as possible to the spirit of the traditional aspects of the art.

In 1992 he travelled to Florida, USA where he underwent training as a pilot and flight Instructor for 2 years, and after successfully completing this returned to the UK for a short while before travelling to the middle-east to train at universities, corporate, and military organisations. Improving his ratings on more complex aircraft.

Receiving an award from the air force for his attitude towards training was testimony to his style, and meeting the President of the country from whom he received his invitation in the first place, one of the highlights. He has provided training and coaching to thousands of staff in the corporate sector.

His anecdotes and real life examples help him get a *"buy in"* from people in a way that is both motivational and exciting

Preface

derived from living and teaching across 3 continents. He enjoys the powerful change in behaviour he instils in people through a unique training style. Frank currently holds the rank of 4th degree black belt in Traditional Shōtōkan Karate and trains 6 days a week, teaching in schools on a daily basis. He also provides karate as an enrichment activity to *Youth Offenders* via the *local County Council* and works with other organisations such as *Connexions* to help teach youngsters self control and discipline via the art.

His military experience gives him a unique insight into knife handling and disengagement. He now shares some of these techniques with the public.

A big part of his time is spent working with *violence* Units helping empower people through Karate. This book is now a product of his time spent with these organisations and provides a guide to Karate for the beginner teaching self defence and also introducing the Japanese culture of training to students who have no knowledge of it.

Making it look so easy!

Introduction

Following the success of the first book it became apparent that there was a need to extend the first edition, but further more a growing interest from the general public to learn the fundamentals of Karate in the first place and how best to tackle street violence. This has been catapulted by the numerous interviews for radio and newspapers' growing fascination in the message I have been trying to get across in a flourishing street crime culture.

Some of the stories I have been listening to nationwide would make an interesting read in their own right.

I have talked to managing directors who recount child abuse at the hands of parents. Mothers speaking of defending children in car parks, in what would seem to be an unprovoked attack. A 15 year old boy named Alfie robbed in broad daylight where the attacker not only demanded he empty his pockets, but then had the audacity to ask the boy, for the time as if late for a meeting, or a favourite programme!

I have talked to member's of a London gang during a bus ride to a book signing event and after enquiring what it took to get into their gang was told shoot someone and you are in!! Plus many more real stories.

How victims deal with violence is the human spirit in action. People have commented how depressing my job is, as I meet and see victims all the time…

On the contrary, it is these individuals who motivate me in life. They are the *"unnamed heroes."* Their stories are not exaggerated but real. They live amongst us, maybe the person sitting next to you on the train or bus?

Introduction

Whilst most have never experienced any type of attack, the sad reality is that 1 in 3 will come across it or have to face a physically confrontational situation at some point during our lives, this is a fact!

Street violence is completely different to domestic violence and a clear distinction needs to be made between the two, as the characteristics of these forms of violence are very different and must be tackled in different ways. Quite often the victim will be living with the abuser and hence self defence is not encouraged as a solution. There are organisations that can specifically help this type of violence.

This manual will explore the fundamentals of Shōtōkan Karate and its direct application, teaching simple yet effective techniques whether a martial artist or not. Preparing the student for grading exams, building confidence and awareness in the process. What is to follow then is my guide as I see it to Defending Against Attack in the only way I know.

It is indeed strange and ironic that an art form which originated thousands of years ago, developed by peasant farmers and monks to protect themselves from bandits is still relevant today.

If you want to learn Karate for obtaining merely a grade there are other books on the market for this. This is teaching self protection and Karate at the same time. It is for the student like myself who always asks questions but does not always get the answers.

The Japanese Bow or Rei

Bowing **(Ojigi)** is a very important custom in Japan. Japanese people bow all the time. Most commonly, they greet each other by bowing instead of handshaking. It is impolite not to return a bow to whoever bowed to you. Japanese people tend to become uncomfortable with any physical forms of contact. But, they understand the need to shake hands with westerners.

Bowing has many functions in one. It expresses the feeling of respect, thanking, apologizing, greeting, and so on. It's a convenient and important custom for you to learn. You can bow, when you say, "Thank you", "Sorry", "Hello", "Good bye", "Congratulations", "Excuse me", "Good night", "Good Morning", and more!!

The Standing Bow

The Japanese Bow or Rei

It depends on the social status or age of the person you bow to. If the person is higher status or older than you are, you should bow deeper and longer. It is polite to bow, bending from your waist. Karate students usually keep their hands in their sides and accompany the *Rei* with the *OSS!*

Furthermore, there are two types of *'Rei'* in Karate. The standing and from the kneeling position. The latter usually following the reciting of the Dōjō Kun (Karate Oaths) which can be found overleaf.

The Kneeling Bow

Dōjō Kun
(Oaths Of The Karate Practitioner)

The Dōjō Kun are the rules of the Dōjō (training place) that have been passed down from Okinawan Karate masters to the present day. Recited at the end of each advanced class, they encompass everything that we are aiming to achieve through the physical efforts of Karate. Make them part of your life not just in the Dōjō.

- ●Hitotsu - Jinkaku kansei ni tsutmuro Koto
- ●Hitotsu - Makoto no michi o mamoru koto
- ●Hitotsu - Do ryoku no seishin o yashinau koto
- ●Hitotsu - Rei gi o omonzuru koto
- ●Hitotsu - Kekki no you o imashi muru koto

- ●One - To strive for The perfection of character!
- ●One - To defend the paths of truth!
- ●One - To foster the spirit of effort!
- ●One - To honour the principles of etiquette!
- ●One - To guard against impetuous courage!

Japanese Version

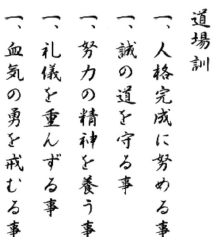

道場訓

一、人格完成に努める事

一、誠の道を守る事

一、努力の精神を養う事

一、礼儀を重んずる事

一、血気の勇を戒むる事

Airborne!

How To Tie Your Karate Belt!

There are several ways of tying your Karate belt or '**Obi**', and this varies from association to association. Entering a training hall the student should be properly dressed for the class. I remember attending a Sensei Kanazawa course (10th Degree black belt) in London where I was horrified to observe a black belt enter the training hall (Dōjō) with his karate belt wrapped around his neck! Tells you a little about the way his classes are run without actually attending one! Needless to say Sensei Kanazawa did not witness this spectacle although I would have been interested to his reaction..

Some Important protocols for tying your belt before, during and after a class:

(i)   Make sure both ends are equal in length
(ii) Always turn away from the instructor and
      class when tying your belt.

1 Kneel over the left leg holding a little to the left

2 Long end wraps round once

How To Tie Your Karate Belt!

3 Then again a second time

4 Adjust both ends so they are equal in length

5 Centre one over the other

6 Top side goes around & through

How To Tie Your Karate Belt!

7   **Pull to tighten and make sure it sits over the waist!**

N.B. Always remember that when another karate practitioner meets you for the first time, those initial impressions are so important. A good way of judging how good a student is by observing them! If you cannot tie your belt what does that say for the rest of your karate?

The History Of Modern Karate-Dō

The Japanese word "kara" translates as **'empty'** and the word "te" means 'hand'. The third word "do" is translated as **'way'**.

Karate-dō is a martial art based upon the principles of self-defence. It was developed on the island of Okinawa by peasants who were denied the possession of weapons by their rulers. In order to defend themselves, the Japanese peasants refined the ancient Chinese fighting methods into a highly effective combat art. Their hands and feet became weapons and through training they were able to defend themselves.

When karate-dō was no longer needed for self protection, it survived as an art form. Since the knowledge and teaching of karate-dō was strictly forbidden by the military government, its masters taught in secrecy. In the 1900's, karate-do was reintroduced to the Japanese people, who refined it for western countries.

Gichin Funakoshi (1868-1957)

was the founder of the Shōtōkan style. Funakoshi was born in the Okinawan capital of Shuri into an upper class family (Shizoku class). Master Gichin Funakoshi was instructed by Yasutsune Azato and Yasutsune Itosu. He was responsible for introducing Karate to Japan in the 1920's.

He changed the 'kara' symbol in Karate from the old symbol, meaning 'China', to the new symbol, meaning 'empty'. In his book *Karate-Do Nyumon*, he writes: "Just as an empty valley can carry a resounding voice, so must the person who follows the Way of Karate make himself void or empty by ridding him-

The History Of Modern Karate-Dō

-self of all self-centeredness and greed. Make yourself empty within, but upright without." This is the real meaning of the 'empty' in Karate.

Today Karate is practiced predominately by children and very few adults come to karate due to the pressures of modern day

living, lack of time and commitment. A sad state of affairs.
In my humble opinion for karate to survive as a fighting system and indeed an 'art form', it must firstly be introduced as self defence to individuals. Once the positive qualities of the discipline become evident I leave it to the individual to decide on it's merits.

Through schools it is being introduced to young adults and it is these students who will become the instructors of tomorrow.

The History Of Modern Karate-Dō

The original teachings of Nakayama Sen-  sei, who was Gichin Funakoshi's most loyal student and head of the famous Japan Karate Association (JKA) of old, are the cornerstone of the my style of Karate. It would be very hard to follow the Shōtō-kan of Gichin Funakoshi today, though the basic principles are the same. Nakayama Sensei moved the system on, making it the most popular dynamic style in the world. Unfortunately, in the early days of Shōtōkan coming to the west, techniques were changed in order to take them easier for the westerner to understand, with a view to teaching the correct form of the techniques once an understanding had been gained. This was a grave mistake, as in many cases the techniques were never corrected, and karate-ka 'perfected' various 'training' techniques. Through the years as Shōtōkan grew and more senior instructors emerged, the original techniques of Shōtōkan seemed to have been forgotten or in some cases never learned in the first place. An example is found in the use of basic blocks. Some instructors just do not understand the technical use or the application, such as their use in attacking or defending.

Another example is the use of front stance, (Please refer to basic techniques and Stances section) in its narrow form (not shoulder width apart), which is very prominent in Nakayama's kata. For certain kata movements, Nakayama taught to pivot on the heels when, for example, moving from kiba dachi to zenkutsu dachi – a technique alien to some senior instructors today.

Introduction To Karate

Karate has never been so relevant than it is in current times. While the emphasis should always be on a non-aggressive response to threatening situations, it is confidence building and empowering to learn a system of techniques and raise general awareness of situations which may facilitate the increase in *'attack chances'*.

Our aim in writing this book is to teach, coach and understand the fundamentals of attack, defensive blocks, and how to avoid danger. Whilst developing the Karate Student.

We will also examine applications for defence based on the Traditional Shōtōkan style of karate, teaching **Basics** (Kihon) **Sparring** (Kumite) and **Formal Exercise** (Kata) with roots originating in Tibet and China dating back hundreds of years!!

Furthermore teaching **Laws Of Etiquette** and building confidence and self esteem through the weekly classes, the student will develop unique physical abilities that help him / her understand their own self-worth in a modern society where discipline and the perfection of the human spirit are attributes very few aim for, as they seem unattainable and beyond reach. Maybe they are but through Karate perhaps we can strive to feed a hunger for it that perhaps did not exist in the first place.

Introduction To Karate

Students expect to reach Black belt almost immediately, and after a demonstration for Karate the uptake is huge for the first class. However this does not last. We lose 20% almost straight away who realise after attending their first session that this may actually involve hard work! Another 10% drop out for reasons more to do with what they expect of training, and what they actually receive. ie. Your are not going to be shown how to break bricks in your first class!

The natural order of attrition takes place and the students who do drop out are the ones who really not suited to this type of training, or actually for want of a better word should not be training. If their reasons in learning karate is to hurt or misuse the knowledge we entrust to them. They do not last. Who becomes a black belt? The average ordinary person who turns up for training regularly, handles rejection without quitting (being human, how well do any of us deal with this?) and struggles to learn the techniques but perseveres!

These are the instructors of tomorrow not the fast learning, naturals who fall by the wayside all too quickly dismissing the art. *When in actual fact the training has just begun...*

1 Eye contact
is key here

2 Attacker grabs the arm
for control

3 Defender rotates up

4 Attacking with the elbow

5 The elbow strikes the chin
forcing the head back

6 Strike to
the face and run!

Introduction To Karate

Mental Awareness Training (MAT)

We will ,refer to these attack reconstructions as attacker and defender, whilst looking at the easiest and safest forms of avoiding attack. So we will concentrate on carefully worked out techniques against targets as are depicted in this book. (Page 54)

The best way to do this is set a *'mental state'* for the level of threat a situation poses.

Comfort Zone is an imaginary area around all of us (usually a distance of one arm's length) where we feel safe in. The moment someone steps into it without our permission it creates tension, and becomes a threat. The usual reaction is to hold the hands up, push the person back, or move back ourselves to recreate the comfort zone. This a normal reaction but wrong and only fuels the attacker, because it is the reaction that is expected. No attacker really considers that they may have picked the wrong person. That will give you an advantage in the assault.

Head Level Roundhouse Kick
Jōdan Mawashi Geri

Introduction To Karate

Mental Awareness Training (MAT)

Increasing your level of alertness and reducing *'attack chances'* relies on preparation and correct avoidance. If something does not feel right it usually isn't! The human body is governed by 5 sensory perceptions:-

Taste, Touch, Smell, Sight, Hearing.

All of which combined together make a formidable force, but the one unaccounted for; *"The sixth sense".* *Is your gut reaction to a situation.* That feeling when you first meet someone and it doesn't feel right? You just not comfortable around them.

Comparing your alertness to the traffic signals has benefits. It gives you a reference point mentally to react to a situation and take action if necessary.

Green state is the condition when you are completely comfortable with someone or in an environment you feel safe in.

Amber state is usually for those split moments when it becomes noticeably unsafe but only for a short moment. This can escalate to red state or drop back down to green.

Red state is in immediate fear of, or in close proximity to an imminent attack. This requires you read the attack, evade or defend yourself.
Switching from one state to another all depends on your reaction and ability to read a situation or person. The more training and interaction you have (in a controlled environment) the better you will become at reading the body language and understanding what is correct behaviour and what is not from a prospective attacker!

Characteristics Of The Attacker
Who is the Attacker?

Attackers do not act out of character but keep to a very orthodox code of attack. This is complicated and may seem odd to the novice. They are relying on your fears and expect certain reactions as a result of those fears. This is positive and negative trauma. To answer this we need to examine and understand 4 types of personality traits in the most common attackers. I have been a victim of the 1 or 2 types of the following and I am sure some of you reading can also relate to one as well!

(i) Scared
(ii) Nervous
(iii) Emotional
(iv) Explosive

The Attacker's Scared (Serious Assault)

This type is someone who is afraid of being hurt or losing something important, or indeed they have already lost something important. Just as a snake will lash out when threatened so does this type of attacker. It's the fear of being hurt that prompts them to violence. This type of defence mechanism is incited through psychological issues and reasoning and ration seems to be futile if not a complete waste of time, however not impossible!

The average person confronted can lack the skills to tackle this type of attacker and in most instances **'backing off'** and keeping eye contact can be a good way of defusing the situation. Lowering your voice helps to calm the situation while abrupt movements can escalate the problem.

Characteristics Of The Attacker
The Attacker's Nervous (Random Assault)

This type is someone who has lost their parameters. They are mentally and emotionally defeated. To regain control, they fight. The feeling being to relieve tension through physical conflict will somehow make things better. This attacker does not choose you through intention but through circumstance. *i.e. you are in the wrong place at the wrong time!*

To de-escalate the situation a assertive tone used with good hand command signals can help the situation.

The Attacker's Emotional (Public Assault)

Emotional attacker is basically a violent person giving a someone a ultimatum : *"Watch out or else"* or *"be quiet and don't say a word or else"* and even *" keep your mouth shout and you won't get hurt"*

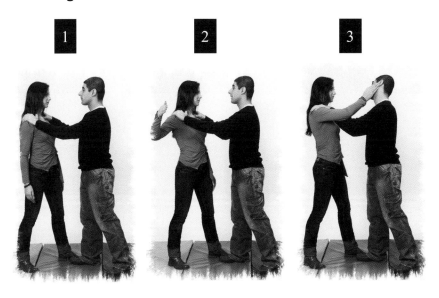

Two Options, Be A Victim Or Fight Back!

Characteristics Of The Attacker

The Attacker's Explosive (Premeditated Assault)

Explosive attacker is different as any excuse will do to attack. Even the most brisk of eye contact which most find unavoidable. It is built up aggression and tension with no release. Like a volcano lying dormant then exploding.

The Explosive attacker is in a constant state of attack mode, meaning they find violence a simple way to calm themselves down. (to avoid exploding) They look for trouble in an attempt to calm down through violence - this attacker is very commonly experience in a violent relationship where everything and anything the wife, girlfriend does only helps to fuel the anger and aggression.

Attacker grabs arm and refuses to release!

Rotate hand around attacker's arm

Characteristics Of The Attacker

The Attacker's Explosive (Premeditated Assault)

Remember they are using you as a means of calming down–
you are a tool or object. (as clinical as this may sound don't
take it personally).
A good counter attack is simply question his intentions and
give him some consequences of those actions.

Positive and Negative Trauma

Earlier on I mentioned attackers relying on certain reactions
from their victims. I will now elaborate on this.

When a random attack takes place as in a theft of a handbag,
the attacker is relying on 3 things to pull off the successful attack:

**With left hand grab attackers
hand**

**Push on the forearm & twist
the hand at the same time**

Characteristics Of The Attacker

- **Element of surprise**
- **Your fear of being hurt (Negative Trauma)**
- **A quick and successful encounter , the chances of attracting attention and getting caught increase the longer the interaction**

While the victim is in a state of negative trauma, the attacker on the other hand is enjoying a state of **'Positive Trauma'**. Everything is going to plan and your reactions only fuel his/her confidence.

The following reactions are Negative Trauma:-

- **Shock**
- **Panic**
- **Noticeable fear**
- **Pleas of begging or whimpering**

These are a few good examples of Positive Trauma which will unnerve the attacker:

- **Calmness**
- **Direct Eye Contact (DEC THE ATTACKER)**
- **Forward motion on your part**

Since attackers are looking for certain reactions any action on your part that causes a negative reaction on theirs will be off putting.

How do you shock an attacker? By (a) not displaying fear and (b) thinking when they expect you to freeze!

Body Tone & Stretching

Teacher learning from the Student!

Body Tone & Stretching

Correctly warming up and stretching the muscles of the body is paramount before any type of physical exercise. In self defence training it becomes even more important bearing in mind the extreme aspects of body use.

What the correct stretching and exercise helps achieve is:-

   (i) *Increases muscle tone* - as you stretch, the muscles will tighten and tone.
   (ii) *Increase flexibility* - which is vital in kicking and avoiding attack.
   (iii) *Increase your heart rate* - In fact a good warm up session should create a sweat. If this is not achieved, well you have not been working hard enough!
   (iv) *Increase your reactions* - being aware of your body's limitations and extremes can help build confidence and increasing your reflexes to a situation because the brain will tell your body what you can and cannot do quicker than before.

Warm up and stretching should not be neglected or indeed taken for granted. It is just as important part of the class. In fact it is the class... but many view it as a prelude to the 'real training'.

Today I spend as much time on my conditioning and body tone as I do on my actual Karate. The older I become the more important these exercises are to maintain the level of fitness and agility required for Karate training.

The techniques that we will learn in the following lesson plans will amount to nothing if the body is not ready to receive it physically.

Body Tone & Stretching

It is also very important that you keep a balance and workout both sides of the body. Your coordination will improve over time. Some you will find more complex than others and you should try and perform them regularly. They get easier the more you practice and regular stretching will help you define and tone muscles without the aid of weights!

Each time you stretch try and push yourself a little further to the last. Bear in mind that in the warm weather your body will feel looser and use this to your advantage to maximise what you get out of your stretching.

'Spirit first, Technique Second!'

Warm-Up & Stretching
(Neck & Shoulders)

Start Position   Turn Left   Turn Right

Start Position   Head Back   Head Forward

Start Position   Right Arm Up   Left Arm up

Warm-Up & Stretching
(Biceps, Triceps & Forearms)

Start Position

Push Down

Push Down

Push Down

Push Down

Stretch Across

Stretch Across

**Right Tricep
Stretch**

**Left Tricep
Stretch**

Warm-Up & Stretching
(Sides & Chest)

Start Position

Left Arm Stretch

Right Arm Stretch

Fold the arms and reach back

Open chest stretch

Make fists to your waist

Join behind and straighten

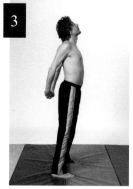

Side view

Warm-Up & Stretching
(Hamstrings & Back)

Left leg across the right

Stretch forward

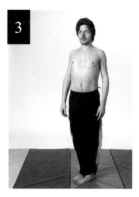

Change right over left

Stretch forward

Up on the heel

Right Elbow down

Up on the heel

Left Elbow down

Warm-Up & Stretching
(Quadriceps and Inner Thighs)

Performing the right side leg stretch, back straight!

Performing the left side leg stretch, back straight!

Soles of the feet together and hands on the ankles

Keeping the back straight now pushing down

Warm-Up & Stretching
(Hamstrings, Calves & Lower back)

1

Performing the right side splits, back straight!

2

Chest forward stretching the hamstrings and the lower back

1

Performing the left side splits, back straight!

2

Chest forward stretching the hamstrings and the lower back

Focusing Power or 'Kime'

One of the more amazing things that anyone observing a typical Shōtōkan class will notice is the way in which body tenses at impact of the technique giving it a sharpness that draws people to the art. The invincibility of the practitioner!

Most people who practice Shōtōkan Karate try their best to move fast and strong in each movement tensing at the execution of the technique.

Some enthusiasts even go so far as tensing their bodies throughout the technique hence slowing the movement down to a maximum. the timing of muscle tensing so that all of the contractions take place at the same time is a finely balanced thing which involves a system of understanding on our part.

 This practice is referred to as 'kime'. In English, the common terminology used is the word - Focus.

There are other meanings for *'focus' or 'kime'*. Notably for karate training, a strong mental condition, putting total effort into your technique so that you follow through with full confidence effort, and technical skill allowing your technique to be devasting at the point of impact causing maximum damage.

Hence the myth behind the saying *'The killer blow'*. It is possible to do this with one punch and you do not need Karate training do so, but the more important question here is:

"Why would you want to, would you not have completely failed in your training?"

Shouting or Kiai!

This is strongly linked to Kime and both play an integral role in the development of both **muscle tension** and **mental concentration**

There are other benefits to shouting at set points in a technique or Kata (Formal Exercise)

Releasing aggression verbally in controlled manner at a set point. Usually prescribed by the instructor through his instruction.

Getting people's attention - I mean here attracting attention as shouting will always do this, referring to a life threatening situation as in street self defence.

From a Shōtōkan Karate point of view it is the ultimate measurement of the **martial spirit** of the practitioner. What does spirit mean?

"Your total physical and mental commitment to a technique manifesting itself verbally with complete emotion, humility, and honesty ."

I often ask students to tell me what the reason was that prompted them to start Karate? The answers vary from the need to learn self defence to confidence building. All of which are good reasons. But surely the ultimate aim;

"Is the perfection of character"

Kihon - Basic Techniques and Stances

There are many considerations in the make of the proficient *'Karateka'* (karate practitioner) in the study of his art. Practice is the only way in which the techniques are mastered not hundreds but thousands of times over many years!

 The Four Elements in shaping the foundation of the Shōtōkan Karate System are -

- **Punching (Zuki)**
- **Kicking (Geri)**
- **Blocking (Uke)**
- **Striking (Uchi)**

However these elements have *roots* called **'Stances'** or **'Dachi'**. If the stances, are strong and correct the karate will develop strong and true. If the roots are weak then this will also reflect in the technique. My students constantly hear me repeating *"bend the knees!"* or *"longer stances, please!"*

A student's enthusiasm in Karate-Dō can be measured through their stances. Long stances indicate positive attributes and short stances negative. Since it is harder to hold a long stance, the easier option is usually employed.

As skill and training increases in frequency, the stances become stronger, (developing muscle and joint strength). In real life combat we do not employ stances. They are a means of developing muscle speed of movement so if we can increase speed when holding a stance surely in normal posture the speed of movement should be so fast whereby the attacker does not see the movement at all! This is the ultimate goal of stance training.

Kihon - Basic Techniques and Stances

The first and foremost stance used in the Shōtōkan system is the **Forward Stance (Zenkutsu Dachi)**. It is the starting position for 98% of the techniques. As skill improves the stances becoming shorter until eventually the normal standing posture is adopted.
The distribution of weight is more forward than back (70/30).

The Forward Stance is a strong hip-width posture. The front knee is bent, and pushing out to strengthen inner thigh muscles. The back leg is slightly bent at the knee to protect the knee and the toes are pointing forward as well to protect the knee again and speed up forward movement.

Kihon - Basic Techniques and Stances

The Back Stance is usually introduced to the student after the rank of 9th Kyu or Red Belt is reached. (Please see section on **Karate Grades** in the closing chapter of this book. **(Page 197)**

Karate stances are performed moving forwards and backwards as in most techniques in our system, but for self defence Bunkai (or application) this stance always feels arguably better on the retreat, which would make sense when we consider. that an aggressor is usually attacking forward.
The distribution of weight is more back than forward (30/70) hence the name Back Stance! The feet are **in-line** as opposed to **'hip width'**

Heels are in–line. Front knee is slightly bent to protect from attack and back is straight over the back leg. The Back Stance is associated with the Knife Hand Block predominately.

Kihon - Basic Techniques and Stances

The Horse Straddle Stance is a very strong stance in that it improves muscle tone and the strengthening of ligaments in the quadriceps and around the Knee area. *The distribution of weight is equal (50/50).* Used heavily in the Tekki Kata's (Formal Exercise). The stance is used as a training and strengthening platform to increase ligament dexterity but also for teaching a number of kicks - Side Thrust & Snap Kicks. Ideal for fighting in corridors and boats where hip width movement is not possible.

Knees bent and back straight. Toes pointing forward and knees pushing out not in. Backside straight. A good way to check your stance is by looking down at your toes and if you can see them over your knees you need to bend the knees more.

Punching & Striking

Punching as a general rule is a tricky affair and even with the most skilled exponent - injury-ridden.

To avoid injury consider what you are punching? How to make a correct fist and use it to punch! The best way to explain this is *hard on soft* and *soft on hard*.

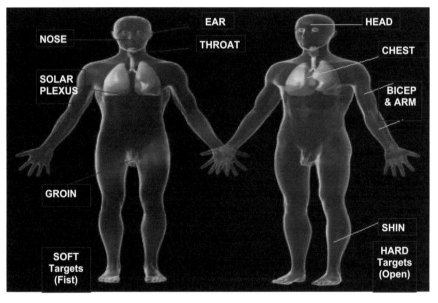

This means fist strikes on soft targets and open hand techniques on hard targets (preferred way).

Striking the soft targets with a fist are effective and will reduce injuries because the fist can withstand the impact of the strike. There are 206 bones in the human body with many nerve points and target areas, to make the learning effective we will be looking at many strike points so your options are not limited.

Punching & Striking

It must be stressed that all of the these strikes points are vulnerable points and I strongly urge readers to study them carefully. The throat being the most vulnerable and hence force applied here must be controlled.

7 Factors

In the execution of techniques the following need to be observed and it is important to note here that without these factors there is only so far a student can develop and no further.

> *•Timing •Form •Balance •Centre Of Gravity •Focus Of Power •Rhythm •Hips •Breathing*

Each of these apply to everything in karate and the ultimate goal for all students is to apply them to techniques automatically and without thinking—as a natural body response.

This mind development over the body helps improve coordination, the creation of new brain cells, and develops student reactions helping to take corrective measures wherever and whenever possible.

We will not be going into too much detail on these needless to say that as you train more the above will make more sense. Better still, the next time your instructor asks if you have any questions why not enquire as to an explanation of one of the above!

Punching & Striking
The Straight Punch & Application - Oi Zuki & Bunkai)

The Straight Punch or Oi–Zuki is the most common of all punches.

The target should be your own solar plexus or nose, until a real target is in front of you. The wrist is kept straight throughout the movement so as to avoid injury or buckling on impact. The Fore knuckles as the point of contact and not the entire fist.

Concentrating a large force into a small area will increase power application to the technique.

**Downward Block /
Gedan Barai**

**Ready / Straight Punch
Yoi / Oi Zuki**

**X Block / Straight Punch
Juji Uke / Oi Zuki**

Punching & Striking
The Straight Punch & Application - Oi Zuki & Bunkai)

Prepare

**Straight Punch /
Oi Zuki**

Step in push arm down

**Right Straight Punch
Migi Oi Zuki**

Punching & Striking
(The Reverse Punch - Gyaku Zuki)

When Punching always pull the opposite arm back to the hips, remember you are punching with the first two knuckles and not the entire fist and breathing in through the nose and out through the mouth on completion.

Shouting as you strike also helps create power in your punch and attract attention! The strike points can be the nose, solar plexus, or the groin. (Please see diagram on page 54)

**Downward Block /
Gedan Barai**

Please also see section on Kiai or Shouting.

***Punch using the first
two fore knuckles not
the entire fist!***

**Forward Stance / Ready position
Zenkutsu Dachi / Yoi**

Punching & Striking
(The Reverse Punch & Application -Gyaku Zuki Bunkai)

Prepare

**Reverse Punch /
Gyaku Zuki**

**Attacking roundhouse kick /
Inside Forearm block
Mawashi Geri / Soto Uchi Uke**

**Reverse Punch /
Gyaku Zuki**

Punching & Striking
(Hook Punch & Application—Yama Zuki & Bunkai)

The hook punch is ideal for close quarter defending when the attacker has either grabbed you or is very close as may be the case in handbag or mobile phone snatch.

The Hook punch allows the defender to put a lot of power behind the punch, and this makes striking to the groin, chin or stomach very effective and painful. Even if you lack physical strength.

Downward Block / Gedan Barai

Downward Block / Ready Gedan Barai / Yoi

Reverse Punch / Palm Heel Block Gyaku Zuki / Teisho Uke

Punching & Striking
(Hook Punch & Application—Yama Zuki & Bunkai)

Prepare

**Hook Punch /
Yama Zuki**

Prepare

**Right Reverse Hook
Punch /
Migi Gyaku Yama Zuki**

Punching & Striking
(The Ridge Hand Strike & Application - Haito Uchi & Bunkai)

The Ridge Hand Strike or Haito Uchi is not a common technique and rarely used but it is so free-flowing & natural to perform in a close quarter fight. The speed of execution is also extremely fast as the technique looks lazy but the thumb closely tucked in makes that ridge hand area very hard and therefore the force of the strike is quite effective. Normally used to strike to the temple or ribs its applications are easy to see for self defence purposes.

Downward Block / Gedan Barai

When teaching a novice beginner the basics the ridge hand is by far the easiest and most natural to teach.

It also makes getting into tight areas like the neck and groin easier as opposed to a fist.

Keep the thumb tucked tightly to harden the ridge hand!

Downward Block / Ready

Punching & Striking
(The Ridge Hand Strike & Application - Haito Uchi &
Bunkai)

Prepare

**Ridge Hand Strike /
Haito Uchi**

Move to the Side / Prepare

Ridge Hand Strike / Haito Uchi

Punching & Striking
(The Knife Hand Strike & Application - Shuto Uchi & Bunkai)

The Knife Hand Strike can be used to attack to the neck or a variety of other target points on the face. It is seldom used in tournaments or basics other than in Kata. But in self defence it's applications become priceless.

The preparation phase should also not be ignored as this stage the extended arm with the hand could also be construed as an attack to the neck or solar plexus.

Thus no preparation phase is wasted in the Shōtōkan System. Everything has a purpose.

Ready Position / Yoi

**Ready / Downward Block
Yoi / Gedan Barai**

**Knife Hand Block / Straight Punch
Shuto Uke / Oi Zuki**

Punching & Striking
(The Knife Hand Strike & Application - Shuto Uchi & Bunkai)

Prepare

**Knife Hand Strike /
Shuto Uke**

Prepare

**Knife Hand Strike
Shuto Uchi**

Left Knife Hand Block in Back Stance -
Hidari Shuto Uke in Kokutsū Dachi

Blocking

There a three rules to blocking correctly:

> ### *'Preparation'*
> *Read the attack correctly!*
> ### *'Timing'*
> *Do not move too early!*
> ### *'Focus of Power'*
> *Use only enough energy to block!*

Since Karate is strictly Self Defence and should only be used in defending against attack, this is going to be a key section in this book. The student learns not only from the instructor but also from Kata (Please see section on Formal Exercise) that every starting technique begins with a defensive block.

Indicating humility, and our strict policy of non-confrontation at all costs. Looking for trouble or offensive behaviour are qualities that do not sit well with the Rules of Karate-Do. (See Dojo Kun, page 20)

In most conflicts the aggression can be diffused through rational conversation and if this is not possible by blocking the attack. It is not always necessary to counter strike. The novice attacker when faced with an experienced practitioner who fends off strikes with blocks will almost immediately realise that they have met their match, choosing one of two options *'quit or run'.*

This surely Is the ultimate aim of any karate student. Damage limitation sounds good to me. In the scheme of things surely better for the practitioner as well.

The guilt of inflicting pain upon another human being are not attributes that many thrive on.

Blocking
(The Downward Block & Application-Gedan Barai & Bunkai)

The downward block is by far the strongest block in Karate. It utilizes the forearm for the blocking action and this means that the defender is using the strongest part of the arm to avoid being hit.

This is key when defending against a large person who is stronger.

To teach coordination to students we start by teaching to move the left leg and as a result the left arm blocks. This is a coordinated block same leg, same arm. The more advanced student will then learn reverse block, whereby the blocking arm is opposite to the leg moving forward or back!

The downward block has many practical applications and the obvious is blocking a kick but it can also be used to disengage from a strong grip!

Ready position / Yoi

Attacker moves in and grabs the arm

Blocking
(The Downward Block & Application-Gedan Barai & Bunkai)

Prepare

**Downward Block /
Gedan Barai**

**Defender disengages
downward block**

**Reverse Punch /
Gyaku Zuki**

Blocking
(The Outside Forearm Block & Application—Soto Ode Uke & Bunkai)

The outside forearm block is the easiest and strongest block in Karate. It utilizes the forearm for the blocking action and this means that the defender is using the strongest part of the arm to avoid being hit.

This is key when defending against a large person.

The right arm blocking uses the right hip to generate power. Almost as if they are both connected and rotating together.

**Downward Block /
Gedan Barai**

The opposite applies if blocking with the left arm.

Block using the fleshy inside part of the forearm!

**Downward Block / Ready position
Gedan Barai / Yoi**

Blocking
(The Outside Forearm Block & Application—Soto Ode Uke & Bunkai)

Prepare

Outside Forearm Block / Soto Ude Uke

Straight Punch / Outside Forearm Block Oi Zuki / Soto Ude Uke

Reverse Punch / Gyaku Zuki

Blocking (Age Uke)
(The Upper Rising Block - Age Uke & Bunkai)

The Upper Rising Block once again utilises the forearm for the blocking action. This block is designed to defend against attacks to the face .

The Upper rising action raising the attackers arm over your head and hence exposing their face, chest and abdomen for a counter strike.

Once again as the arm lifts up to block so should the opposite arm return straight back to the hip. This opposite action and reaction of the arms is where the technique develops power and speed from.

The uprising action can also be a strike under the chin or used to break the arm above the elbow joint. Depends on your application!

**Downward Block /
Gedan Barai**

**Downward Block / Ready
Gedan Barai**

> **Push the hip forward to match the arm blocking**

Blocking (Age Uke)
(The Upper Rising Block - Age Uke & Bunkai)

2

Prepare

3

**Uprising Block /
Age Uke**

2

3

**Straight Punch / Uprising Block
Oi Zuki / Age Uke**

**Reverse Punch /
Gyaku Zuki**

Punching & Striking
(Teishō Uchi—The Palm Heel Strike- Teishō Uke)

The Palm Heel Strike has many applications, it can be used to strike a variety of targets and can easily be adapted to blocks as well.

Commonly striking across the face, but what makes this technique so much more effective is the target area rather than the force applied.

If it is used above the elbow joint to block a punch it will inevitably break the arm. Force is more important that the speed of the technique.

1

Downward Block / Gedan Barai

1

Inhale on preparation and exhale on execution!

Downward Block / Ready Gedan Barai / Yoi

Punching & Striking
(Teishō Uchi—The Palm Heel Strike- Teishō Uke)

2

Prepare

3

**Palm Heel Strike /
Teishō Uchi**

2

**Reverse Punch / Palm Heel
Strike
Gyaku Zuki / Teisho Uchi**

*Strike above the
elbow joint and the
arm will break!*

Blocking
(The X-Block & Applications- Jūji Uke Bunkai)

The X Block is a very strong block meeting force with force and usually employed against the front kick as in the Bunkai below. It can be performed at two levels, upper and lower.

(There is an application for this kick demonstrating the Upper Level X Block later in this manual).

The technique does not move the defender away from the attacker but keeps him/her very close to the action, thus the counter has to be swift and final.

Ready Position / Yoi

Forward Stance / Ready Position Zenkutsu Dachi / Yoi

Preparation

Blocking
(The X-Block - Jūji Uke Bunkai)

Prepare

**X Block /
Juji Uke**

**X Block /
Juji Uke**

**Backfist /
Uraken**

Punching & Striking
(The Knife Hand Block & Application - Shuto Uke & Bunkai)

The Knife Hand Block can be used to block against leg and more commonly punch attacks. It is seldom used in tournaments other than in Basics and Kata applications. But in self defence it's effectiveness becomes priceless.

The preparation phase should also not be ignored as this stage the extended arm with the hand could also be construed as an attack to the neck or solar plexus.

Thus no technique or preparation phase is wasted in the Shōtōkan System.

**Ready Position /
Yoi**

**Ready / Downward Block
Yoi / Gedan Barai**

**Knife Hand Block / Straight
Punch
Shūto Uke / Oi Zuki**

Punching & Striking
(The Knife Hand Block & Application - Shuto Uke & Bunkai)

Prepare

Knife Hand Strike / Shuto Uke

Please also refer to the Formal Exercise section where more applications are shown for this technique. The Knife Hand Block is a very difficult technique to master.

If we look at all the elements:

(i) There is the back stance which on its own is extremely difficult.

(ii) The Blocking Arm forms a right angle and the finger tips should be no higher than the shoulders.

(iii) The supporting arm forms a horizontal line, on the solar plexus the technique derives its power like all Karate techniques from the stomach or 'Hara' - consider this the engine power plant to your techniques! Without it there is no power!

Kicking

A Roundhouse Kick Head Level / Jōdan Mawashi Geri

Kicking

A Side Thrust Kick With A Smile!
(Yoko Geri Kekomi)

Kicking

Kicking allows the exponent to keep a safe distance from the attacker as a result of a greater reach compared to the arms. An immediate advantage when fighting a taller person.

I am fortunate to have trained with very skilled exponents of the Shōtōkan Karate System, and as a result the following pages will teach the correct way to deliver a variety of kicks. Not for the novice student and only really introduced after a basic understanding of the stances and blocking and punching techniques have been grasped.

Kicking can be extremely enjoyable to learn or frustrating de-pending on the body type and agility of the student. Some make it look easy whilst others have to work at it for many years. All can however learn to execute them to a certain de-gree with **accuracy, power and consistency**.

Now just as we will learn to kick it is also important to note when you are likely to be kicked? This usually occurs once the victim has been knocked to the floor, as most attackers are both cowards and lazy hence bending over is too much hard work, and will be avoided wherever possible.

Kicking demonstrates confidence as well. Students with natural agility will always prefer to use their legs in tournaments. The speed of a kick also can be very well developed once the basic technique has been enhanced and practiced over the years.

For self defence the attacker will be rarely expecting a kick as a counter. Very few people defend against an attack using legs thus the first time it is experienced - the attacker is caught completely off guard!

Kicking

The following kicks apply to our system:

Front Kick - Mae Geri
Stamp Kick - Fumi Komi
Knee Kick - Heza Geri
Side Thrust Kick- Yoko Geri Kekomi
Roundhouse Kick - Mawashi Geri
Reverse Roundhouse Kick - Ushiro Mawashi Geri
Crescent Kick - Mikazuki Geri

Although kicking may seem very destructive, I hope that we can not only look at them as a means of striking but also blocking. The crescent kick being a good example of one which can be used to block a punch or another kick!

Kicking (Mae Geri)
(The Front Kick & Application - Mae Geri Bunkai)

The front kick is arguably the most executed in tournaments, practice and in the street effort. This does not make it simple however.

The key step is the knee. The higher the knee the stronger and higher the kick. Striking areas here are the stomach, groin or face.

The snapping action of the leg makes it difficult for the leg to be grabbed allowing the student to hit the target and repel, leaving the opponent dazed, confused and in pain!

Downward Block / Gedan Barai

Defender raises the left arm

Attacker grabs the throat and threatens with a fist

Kicking (Mae Geri)
(The Front Kick & Application- Mae Geri Bunkai)

Prepare

**Front Kick /
Mae Geri**

**She slams her forearm down
on the attackers arm**

**Applies a kick into the
groin**

Kicking (Fumikomi)
(The Stamp Kick & Application- Fumikomi Bunkai)

This is a perfect kick for distracting any attacker who grabs from behind, it can be used to disengage the grip, namely through pain, but also inflict heavy damage to the instep of the foot.

Most shoes will be heavily padded on the soles and heels but very few have padding on top. This is where you are aiming your heel at.

If you are wearing high heels shoes concentrating the stiletto heel into target will probably break the foot.

**Forward Stance /
Zenkutsu Dachi**

**Facing away as in getting
into a car or at a cash point**

Attacker grabs from behind

Kicking (Fumikomi)
(The Stamp Kick & Application- Fumikomi Bunkai)

Prepare

**Stamp Kick /
Fumikomi**

Raise the knee

**Check target and apply
full down force through
the heel**

Kicking (Hiza Geri)
(The Knee Kick & Application - Hiza Geri & Bunkai)

The strongest kick in Karate which takes very little effort in performing to generate power. Merely the raising of the Knee to the target is enough to cause pain.

The target area is the abdomen once again, the Solar plexus and groin seemed to be made for this kick.

As the knee rises the toes are pointing down to help give the knee a focal point.

Breathing in through the nose and exhaling through the mouth also help give the kick energy and power.

This is a close quarter kick as in strangle, throat and arm holds.

**Downward Block /
Gedan Barai**

Toes pointing down on the kick will help focus power!

**Ready Position / Downward Block
Yoi / Gedan Barai**

Kicking (Hiza Geri)
(The Knee Kick & Application - Hiza Geri & Bunkai)

**Knee Kick /
Hiza Geri**

**Uprising Block / Straight Punch
Age Uke / Oi Zuki**

**Grab the Head and Knee
Kick / Hiza Geri**

Kicking
(Side Thrust Kick & Application - Yoko Geri Kekomi Bunkai)

**Horse Straddle Stance /
Kiba Dachi**

Prepare

The Thrust Kick or Yoko Geri Kekomi is designed with knee joints in mind. It seems too powerful to be wasted against a soft target (abdomen). For a self defence application striking across the knee joint would seem much more plausible, against an attacker with a knife stopping him in his tracks.

> **Turn the supporting heel to the target area**

**Freestyle Position /
Jiyu Dachi**

Kicking
(Side Thrust Kick & Application - Yoko Geri Kekomi Bunkai)

Prepare

**Side Thrust kick /
Yoko Geri Kekomi**

**Reverse Downward Block /
Thrust Kick
Gyaku Gedan Barai / Kekomi**

**Side Thrust kick Head
level /
Yoko Geri Kekomi Jōdan**

Kicking
(Round House Kick & Application - Mawashi Geri)

The roundhouse kick a favourite at tournaments is an extremely difficult kick to execute and injury ridden if taught incorrectly.

The main consideration is preparation as in all kicks. The rotation of the supporting leg (on the ball of the foot) and the twisting of the hip over the kick . The higher the knee rises at the preparation phase the higher the kick delivered.

**Forward Stance /
Zenkutsu Dachi**

This kick can be used to attack the ribs or head depending on the student and it is a extremely fast technique once mastered. In kickboxing it is used to strike at the legs using the shin as an attack area. In Karate we use the ball of the foot to attack with, & in tournaments purely for safety reasons the instep. The toes should always be curled up as striking with this part will almost always break them.

*The higher the Knee
The higher the Kick*

Ready Position / Downward Blo

Kicking
(Round House Kick & Application - Mawashi Geri Bunkai)

Prepare

**Roundhouse Kick /
Mawashi Geri**

Inside Forearm Block / Straight Punch

Roundhouse Kick /

Kicking
(Reverse Round House Kick & Application - Ushiro Mawashi Geri Bunkai)

The reverse roundhouse kick a favourite of tournaments but extremely difficult to execute and injury ridden if taught incorrectly.

The main consideration is preparation as in all kicks. The rotation of the supporting leg (on the ball of the foot) and the twisting of the hip over the kick . The higher the knee rises at the preparation phase the higher the kick delivered.

This kick can be used to attack the knee, ribs or head depending on the student and is an extremely fast technique once mastered.

Forward Stance / Zenkutsu Dachi

Ready Position / Downward Block Yoi / Gedan Barai

Front Kick / X Block Mae Geri / Juji Uke

Kicking
(Reverse Round House Kick & Application - Ushiro Mawashi Geri Bunkai)

Prepare

Reverse Roundhouse Kick / Ushiro Mawashi Geri

Prepare

Reverse Roundhouse Kick / Ushiro Mawashi Geri

Kicking
(Crescent Kick & Application - Mikazuki Geri & Bunkai)

The Crescent kick is the least practiced kick in the Shōtōkan system. Dismissed as too fancy and lacking power and application.

A huge mistake. It can be used to block a punch, or kick, or attack the chest, head, ribs or knees.

On second thoughts maybe not so easy after all.

The motion for travel for this kick varies as compared to the roundhouse. Namely the hip does not rise above the kick. Instead it stays where it is and the rotation of the supporting leg is pretty much minimal. This results in a very fast action and is effective against a larger opponent with a longer reach where blocking with the arms brings you too close to the opponent.

**Forward Stance /
Zenkutsu Dachi**

**Ready / Downward Block
Yoi / Gedan Barai**

Kicking
(Crescent Kick & Application - Mikazuki Geri & Bunkai)

2

**Right Crescent Kick /
Migi Mikazuki Geri**

> ***Practice the kick first
> then concentrate on
> height!***

2

**Crescent Kick Block /
Mikazuki Geri**

3

**Crescent Kick /
Mikazuki Geri**

Upper Elbow Strike
Age Empi Uchi

Sparring (Kumite)

Sparring (Kumite) is the training method whereby the practical application of techniques for defence and attack can be put to the test.

It allows the student to pair up with another of varying body height, type and weight and develop strong blocks and counter attacks using live targets in a controlled system of training. The advantages and emphasis are training with as many different people as possible to prepare the student for understanding the accuracy, timing and distancing required to defend oneself in a live scenario where avoidance measures are not possible. Kumite starts in basic forms and develops with grade and ability to final stage of free sparring which is the closest assimilation to real combat as possible. we will concentrate on:

Gohon Kumite - (Five Attack Sparring) Jōdan & Chudan

It is a form of practice in which the stances, targets, blocks, counters, and strikes are all prearranged.

Kihon Ippon Kumite - (One Attack Sparring) Sets 1-5

The main difference between this and the basic kumite exercises is that the exchange is now limited to only one attack. This means that the opportunity afforded for a second chance in the basic levels of kumite has been eliminated. This is now the more realistic option for self defence applications as the argument here is for real life attack the encounter would be over in a matter of seconds not minutes as us portrayed in movies.

There are other more advanced forms of Kumite (*Jiyu, Okuri Kumite*) but until the above are mastered, and their applications learned, there is no need in showing others at this stage.

Gohon Kumite - (Five Attack Sparring)
Jōdan (Upper Level)

Left Uprising Block / Right Punch
Hidari Age Uke / Migi Oi Zuki

Right Uprising Block / Left Punch
Migi Age Uke / Hidari Oi Zuki

The Movements (6) and (7) are performed as one. The feeling being Block and Counter.

Right Reverse Punch
Migi Gyaku Zuki

Gohon Kumite - (Five Attack Sparring)
Jōdan (Upper Level)

Left Uprising Block / Right Punch
Hidari Age Uke / Migi Oi Zuki

Ready / Downward Block
Yoi / Gedan Barai

Left Uprising Block / Right Punch
Hidari Age Uke / Migi Oi Zuki

Right Uprising Block / Left Punch
Migi Age Uke / Hidari Oi Zuki

Gohon Kumite - (Five Attack Sparring) Chudan (Middle Level)

Right Outside Forearm Block / Left Punch Migi Soto Ude Uke/ Hidari Oi Zuki

Left Outside Forearm Block / Right Punch Hidari Soto Ude Uke/ Migi Oi Zuki

The Movements (5) and (6) are performed as one. The feeling being Block and Counter.

Gohon Kumite - (Five Attack Sparring)
Chudan (Middle Level)

Right Outside Forearm Block / Left Punch Migi Soto Ude Uke/ Hidari Oi Zuki

Left Outside Forearm Block / Right Punch Hidari Soto Ude Uke/ Migi Oi Zuki

Right Reverse Punch Migi Gyaku Zuki

Left Outside Forearm Block / Right Punch Hidari Soto Ude Uke/ Migi Oi Zuki

Kihon Ippon Kumite
(One Attack Sparring) Sets 1

Jōdan (Head Level Attack)

Yoi / Gedan Barai   Age Uke / Oi Zuki   Gyaku Zuki

Chūdan (Middle Level Attack)

Yoi / Gedan Barai   Soto Ude Uke /   Gyaku Zuki
Oi Zuki

Kihon Ippon Kumite
(One Attack Sparring) Set 1

Mae Geri (Front Snap Kick)

Yoi / Zenkutsu Dachi   Gedan Barai /   Gyaku Zuki
                      Mae Geri

N.B. THIS SECTION WILL FOCUS ON COMPLETE JAPA-
NESE TERMINOLOGY SINCE AT THIS STAGE OF TRAIN-
ING INCREASING VOCABULARY IS KEY. (PLEASE USE
GLOSSARY AT THE BACK OF THE BOOK IF UNSURE)

> **Both sides should Kiai on attack and counter.**
> **Demonstrating martial spirit.**

Kihon Ippon Kumite
(One Attack Sparring) Set 2

Jōdan (Head Level Attack)

| Yoi / Gedan Barai | Tate Shuto Uke / Oi Zuki | Mawashi Shūto Uchi |

Chūdan (Middle Level Attack)

Yoi / Gedan Barai   MIgi Soto Ude Uke   Prepare

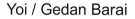

Kihon Ippon Kumite
(One Attack Sparring) Set 2

Mae Geri (Front Snap Kick)

Yoi / Zenkutsu Dachi   Gyaku Gedan Barai   Kizami Zuki

Chūdan (continued)

Kiai!

Gyaku Zuki

Empi in
Kiba Dachi

> **Kizami Zuki**
> **Jab / Stun Punch**

Kihon Ippon Kumite
(One Attack Sparring) Set 3

Jōdan (Head Level Attack)

Yoi / Gedan Barai   Age Uke   Yoko Geri Keage
                                                             Side Snap Kick

Kiai!

Prepare   Empi Uchi

Kihon Ippon Kumite
(One Attack Sparring) Set 3

Chūdan (Middle Level Attack)

Soto Uchi Uke   Kizami Zuki   Gyaku Zuki

Mae Geri (Front Snap Kick)

Juji Uke   Prepare   Juji Uchi

Kihon Ippon Kumite
(One Attack Sparring) Set 3

Kekomi (Thrust Kick)

Yoi / Zenkutsu Dachi   Soto Ude Uke /   Gyaku Zuki
Kekomi

Mawashi Geri (Roundhouse Kick)

Yoi / Zenkutsu Dachi   Soto Uchi Uke   Chūdan
Nukite

Kihon Ippon Kumite
(One Attack Sparring) Set 4

Jōdan (Head Level Attack)

Yoi / Gedan Barai

Jōdan Juji Uke / Oi Zuki

Kiai!

Mawashi Geri / Oi Zuki

Mawashi Empi

Jōdan - Head Level
Chūdan– Middle Level
Gedan - Lower Level

Kihon Ippon Kumite
(One Attack Sparring) Set 4

Chūdan (Middle Level Attack)

Yoi / Gedan Barai

Shūto Uke

Mae Geri

Chūdan Nukite

Nukite
Spear Hand Strike

Kihon Ippon Kumite
(One Attack Sparring) Set 4

Mae Geri (Front Snap Kick)

Yoi / Gedan Barai

Gedan Barai / Mae Geri

Tate Shūto Uke

Mawashi Empi Uchi

Strike Point with the Elbow is the Chin or Solar Plexus depending on height!

Kihon Ippon Kumite
(One Attack Sparring) Set 4

Kekomi (Thrust Kick)

Yoi / Gedan Bari

Mawashi Gedan Uke

Haito Uchi

Always consider each attack as fatal and therefore your block needs to be equal to the force being applied, but no more. Why waste energy and time!

Kihon Ippon Kumite
(One Attack Sparring) Set 4

Mawashi Geri (Roundhouse kick)

Gedan Barai / Yoi

Prepare

Mawashi Geri /
Morote Tate
Shuto Uke

Prepare

Empi Uchi

Kihon Ippon Kumite
(One Attack Sparring) Set 5

Jōdan (Head Level Attack)

Yoi / ZenKutsu Dachi

Age Uke / Oi Zuki

Mae Geri

Kiai!

Age Empi Uchi

Uprising Elbow Striking under the chin!

Kihon Ippon Kumite
(One Attack Sparring) Set 5

Chūdan (Middle Level Attack)

Yoi / Gedan Barai   Blocking   Mawashi Empi Uchi

Mae Geri (Front Snap Kick)

Yoi / Gedan Barai   Sequi Uke / Mae Geri   Chūdan Nukite

Kihon Ippon Kumite
(One Attack Sparring) Set 5

Kekomi

Yoi / Gedan Barai

Gedan Barai / Kekomi

Chūdan Kekomi

> **Always keep an eye on the opponent, even after the conflict is over!**

Kihon Ippon Kumite
(One Attack Sparring) Set 5

Mawashi Geri

1

Yoi / Gedan Barai

2

Mawashi Geri /
Soto Ude Uke

3

Mae Geri

4

Kiai!

Chūdan Gyaku Zuki

Formal Exercise

Kata is the Japanese word for the traditional formal exercise in Karate. They are formulated into patterns and consist of sequence of movements both defensive and offensive against an imaginary person. All kata begin and end with a Rei (bow) and should end in the same position you started from. By learning kata you are walking in the footsteps of the masters and historically the handing down of knowledge in karate was achieved through kata from one generation to the next before being documented and recorded as it has been today.

From a physical point of view kata helps strengthen bone and muscle while from a mental one it helps mind, body and spirit through practice heightening awareness. Correct breath control and focus through Kiai (shouting at set points to demonstrate martial spirit and release aggression) help intensify the power of the techniques. All kata begin and end with a defensive technique stressing the aim that self defence and the use of Karate serves a defensive role and should only be used as a last resort in the circumstance of extreme unprovoked attack cannot be avoided by any means.

They also allow students to practise alone without the need for any special equipment, and help relieve stress. Every movement has a meaning, there are no superfluous actions Each Kata tells us a little about the Master who created them.

The spirit in which they are demonstrated should remain true to the original teachings of the masters who devised them. Through regular training and repetition.

Formal Exercise

If Kata are performed confidently the student may eventually understand why they were devised in the first place. Kata therefore explain a great deal about the times in which they were created. The more we study there applications the greater the learning becomes.

For each Kata the student should try to visualise the application for each movement. If it is a striking technique where we are striking to? And if it is a blocking one, what we are blocking against?

Once the basic concept of visualisation is attained the student no longer becomes aware of their surroundings but sees only the attackers that they are either defending from or counter striking against. A form of meditation! Without the chanting!

The advanced student should then not only try to visualise the applications but have in mind at least 3 different Bunkai (applications) for each technique. Thus the learning becomes more engrossing and stops despondency or boredom as a result! Something I have never grown tired of in 26 years.

Each Kata is unique and in providing applications for the techniques. We will introduce the most common applications. Rather than spoon feed the reader as to every application I leave a little room for the student to try and discover their own scenarios.

After all the only way the Kata truly becomes *'yours'* is to take ownership of it through the repetition of the movements. Practice really does make perfect!

Formal Exercise
Takaiyoku Shōdan (First Cause)

Start Position	**Yoi**	**Prepare**	**Left Downward Block**
Prepare	**Left Downward Block**	**Right Straight Punch**	**Left Straight Punch**
Prepare	**Right Downward Block**	**Left Straight Punch**	**Prepare**
Prepare	**Left Downward Block**	**Right Straight Punch**	**Prepare**

Formal Exercise
Takaiyoku Shōdan (First Cause)

4 Right Straight Punch	**P** Prepare	**5** Right Downward Block	**6** Left Straight Punch
10 Right Straight Punch *Kiai!*	**P** Prepare	**11** Left Downward Block	**12** Right Straight Punch *Kiai!*
15 Left Downward Block	**16** Right Straight Punch	**17** Left Straight Punch	**18** Right Straight Punch
21 Right Downward Block	**22** Left Straight Punch	**23** Stop Yame	**24** Start Position

Formal Exercise Applications
Takaiyoku Shōdan Bunkai

**Defender performs
Downward block**

**Reverse Punch /
Gyaku Zuki**

**Defender performs downward
block slightly differently**

**Using it as a
downward strike!**

Vertical Ridge Hand Block
Tate Shūto Uke

Formal Exercise
Heian Shodan (Peaceful Mind Level One)

Start Position

Ready

Prepare

Left Downward Block

Left Straight Punch

Prepare

Left Downward Block

Prepare

Right Uprising Block

Prepare

Left Downward Block

Right Straight Punch

Left Downward Block

Right Straight Punch

Left Straight Punch

Right Straight Punch

Formal Exercise
Heian Shodan (Peaceful Mind Level One)

Right Straight Punch

Prepare

Right Downward Block

Bottom Fist Strike

Right Uprising Block

Prepare

Left Uprising Block

Prepare

Prepare

Right Downward Block

Left Straight Punch

Prepare

Prepare

Left Knife Hand Block

Prepare

Right Knife Hand Block

Formal Exercise
Heian Shodan (Continued…...)

Prepare   **Right Knife**   **Prepare**   **Left Knife**
              Hand Block   **Hand Block**

Yame   **Start Position**

Formal Exercise
Heian Nidan (Peaceful Mind Level Two)

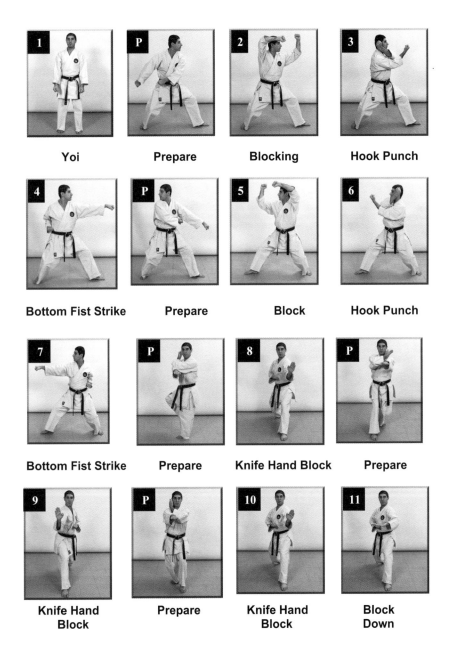

Yoi	Prepare	Blocking	Hook Punch
Bottom Fist Strike	Prepare	Block	Hook Punch
Bottom Fist Strike	Prepare	Knife Hand Block	Prepare
Knife Hand Block	Prepare	Knife Hand Block	Block Down

Formal Exercise
Heian Nidan (Peaceful Mind Level Two)

Spear Hand Strike   Knife Hand Block   Knife Hand Block   Knife Hand Block

Knife Hand Block   Prepare   Ridge Hand Block   Inside Forearm Block

Front Kick   Reverse Punch   Inside Forearm Block   Front Kick

Reverse Punch   Inside Forearm Block   Augmented Forearm Block   Downward Block

Formal Exercise
Heian Nidan (Peaceful Mind Level Two)

| Prepare | Uprising Block | Prepare | Downward Block |

Kiai!

| Prepare | Uprising Block | Yame | Start Position |

Techniques 17—24 Front View

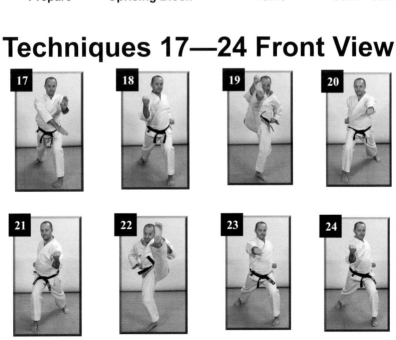

Formal Exercise
Heian Nidan Bunkai

Movements 2-3-4

Blocking Forearm Block
augmented

Inside Hook Punch

**Bunkai must work!
Try to devise at least one
application for every
technique!**

Bottom Fist Strike to
the neck or temple

Formal Exercise Applications
Heian Nidan Bunkai

Movement 8

Straight Punch / Prepare

Back Fist Block

Side Snap Kick

Turn with Elbow
strike to the Solar
plexus

Formal Exercise
Heian Sandan (Peaceful Mind Level Three)

1 Yoi

2 Prepare

3 Inside Forearm Block

P Kosa Uke

4 Kosa Uke

P Prepare

5 Kosa Uke

P Prepare

6 Inside Forearm Block

P Prepare

7 kosa Uke

P Prepare

8 Augmented Forearm Block

9 Palm Heel Block

P = Preparation Movement
Prepare - Breathe in
Execute - Breathe out

Formal Exercise
Heian Sandan (Peaceful Mind Level Three)

Spear Hand Strike   **Rotate**   **Back Fist**   **Prepare**

Kiai!

Straight Punch   **Prepare**   **Crescent Kick**   **Elbow Block**

Back Fist   **Prepare**   **Rotate**   **Crescent Kick**

Elbow Block   **Back Fist**   **Prepare**

Formal Exercise
Heian Sandan

Crescent Kick   **Elbow Block**   **Back Fist**   **Prepare**

Vertical Block   **Rotation Across**   **Prepare**   **Straight Punch**

Pull up   **Rotate**   **Left Punch**   **Right Punch**

Yame   **Starting Position**

Yoi means 'Ready'
Yame means 'Stop'

Formal Exercise Applications
Heian Sandan

Techniques 3—6 Front View

Inside Forearm
Block

Step Up Right
Arm Forward

Left Arm On
Right Shoulder

Inside Forearm
/ Downward Block

Right Arm to
Left Shoulder

Inside Forearm/
Downward Block

P = Preparation Technique

Formal Exercise Applications
Heian Sandan Bunkai

Movements 1-2-3-4

Look first, then move   Inside Forearm Block

Straight punch to   Back Fist Strike
abdomen   to the temple

Formal Exercise
Heian Yondan (Peaceful Mind Level Four)

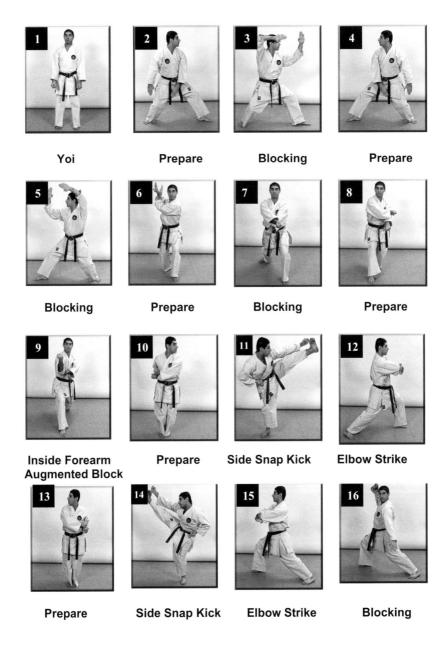

Yoi

Prepare

Blocking

Prepare

Blocking

Prepare

Blocking

Prepare

Inside Forearm
Augmented Block

Prepare

Side Snap Kick

Elbow Strike

Prepare

Side Snap Kick

Elbow Strike

Blocking

Formal Exercise
Heian Yondan

Striking	**Front Kick**	**Prepare**	**Striking**
Prepare	**Blocking**	**Front Kick**	**Straight Punch**
Prepare	**Blocking**	**Prepare**	**Straight Punch**
Reverse Punch	**Prepare**	**Augmented Block**	**Prepare**

Formal Exercise
Heian Yondan (Peaceful Mind Level Four)

Augmented Block **Prepare** **Augmented Block** **Grabbing**

Kiai!

Knee Kick **Prepare** **Knife Hand Block** **Prepare**

Knife Hand Block **Yame** **Starting position**

Formal Exercise Applications
Heian Yondan Bunkai

Movements

Blocking Augmented
Inside forearm block

Grab the neck

Pull down with Knee
kick to face

Turn with elbow strike
to Solar Plexus

Formal Exercise
Heian Godan (Peaceful Mind Level 5)

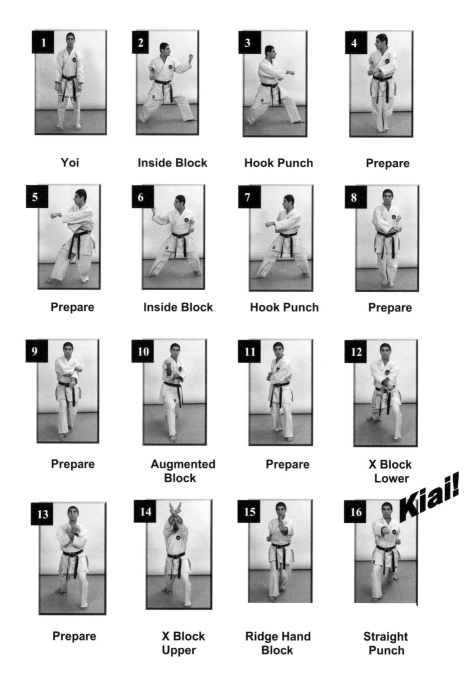

1 Yoi	**2** Inside Block	**3** Hook Punch	**4** Prepare
5 Prepare	**6** Inside Block	**7** Hook Punch	**8** Prepare
9 Prepare	**10** Augmented Block	**11** Prepare	**12** X Block Lower
13 Prepare	**14** X Block Upper	**15** Ridge Hand Block	**16** Straight Punch

Kiai!

Formal Exercise
Heian Godan (Peaceful Mind Level 5)

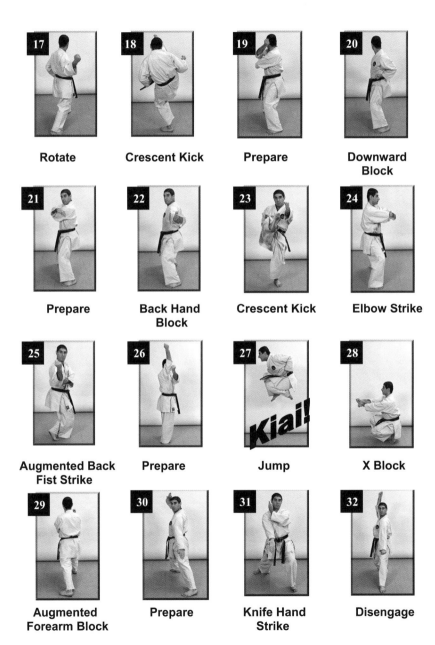

17 Rotate	**18** Crescent Kick	**19** Prepare	**20** Downward Block
21 Prepare	**22** Back Hand Block	**23** Crescent Kick	**24** Elbow Strike
25 Augmented Back Fist Strike	**26** Prepare	**27** Jump	**28** X Block
29 Augmented Forearm Block	**30** Prepare	**31** Knife Hand Strike	**32** Disengage

Formal Exercise
Heian Godan (Peaceful Mind Level 5)

Pull Up

Prepare

Downward Block

Knife Hand Strike

Disengage

Breathe In

Yame

Starting Position

Bow

Formal Exercise Applications
Heian Godan Bunkai

Movements 1-2-3

Blocking Inside Forearm Block
In Back Stance

Hook Punch
right hip in with punch

> *Rather than break the arm movement (3) can be used to lower the face for a Left Front kick!*

Rotate and pull tight to
trap and break arm

Formal Exercise Applications
Heian Godan Bunkai

Movements 12-16

X Block

Pull back

X Block

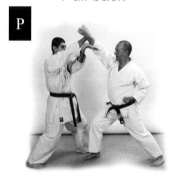

Rotate Hands

Push Down

Straight Punch

Multiple Attackers & Evasion

How do you Control an attacker?

Controlling attackers refers to the gripping, handling of an opponent typically through the application of various counterholds and strikes. You can do this both from a standing position, and on the ground.

When unskilled fighters get embroiled in combat, a common reaction is to grab the opponent in an attempt to slow the situation down by holding them still, resulting in an unsystematic struggle that relies on brute force. A skilled fighter, in contrast, can perform takedowns and evasion as a way of progressing to a superior position.

As we are generally looking at men attacking women it is safe to assume but not always the case by any stretch of the imagination that the attacker will normally be stronger.

So we need to look at techniques that allow the victim of the attack (I use this term loosely as the attacker has made you a victim rather than through choice) to parry, evade and avoid harm by using the opponents strength against him.

Defending against multiple attackers raises a different defence programme. Namely meeting force with **good timing, and speed** keeping the end result in mind, to escape without injury. Put simply get rid of the threat in order of the danger it poses.

This system of defence is best covered through Aikido roughly translated *'The way to perfect harmony'*. Watching it in action you can see how effective it is for dealing with numerous attackers.

Multiple Attackers & Evasion

Being knocked to the ground is very common in the home but can happen outside in the street. If it happens do not lose heart or panic as the only way an attacker can get to you is by coming down to your level. Alternatively they are actually restricted as to what they can attack you with, namely a kick.

Karate promotes healthy physical interaction between two persons as long as it is supervised and both parties start with slow role play to simulate attack and defences. If you prefer to train with people of the same sex I find this beneficial but would strongly advise against it, as a mixed class will always be more realistic and you are likely to have a better interaction.

Also avoid training with the same partner every week. Over a period of time you get to know each other so well that the fighting becomes unrealistic. Try and change partners and train with as many people as possible in a class. Each will have something unique about them that you will find challenging and since no 2 attackers are the same the learning is huge.

Multiple Attackers & Evasion

Both attackers grab hold of each arm

Defender turns and kicks attacker 1 in the groin

Defender applies strike to throat with control

What comes next up to you?

Multiple Attackers & Evasion

Attacker 1 grabs neck

Defender pushes into the throat

Defender applies left hand strike to the groin

Defender now strikes

Multiple Attackers & Evasion

Fighting off one attacker is hard enough at the best of times, but what happens when you are faced with two or more assailants?

There is no quick and easy answer for this. My best advice would be to run if possible. If this is not an option there are some basic observations to consider and I am speaking from experience. Firstly the assailant that is the closest to you is not always the biggest threat. The quickest way to get rid of the threat is prioritise your workload.

Which one poses the greatest threat to you? In most instances the ring leader is usually the one doing all of the talking. He is not likely to be the first to attack. Hs job is to give the others the courage to attack, almost like motivating them with a pep talk. He also has a second role divert your attention to him and not to the actual attack. The **'Quiet Assailant'** is the one who is concentrating on attacking.

He cannot mutli-task so he is working out what he is going to do. Hence he is quiet! When the first person attacks the others usually follow very quickly to aid their colleague.

Multiple Attackers & Evasion

Why? Well if they were brave enough to fight on their own they would have and not in a group.

The key here is not to get tangled up in the conflict but be decisive with a **'Block and Counter'** strategy. The counter has to stop the attacker because you will need to divert your attention to the next one very quickly. Once the assailants realise that you are a tougher target than expected the egos and courage starts to disappear. The attack cycle diminishes.

Even after striking the first attacker look for an exit route and run if you can. If not, work your way out of a bad situation.

I was once faced with a group of youths in a park who surrounded me and a similar situation presented itself . One was **the talker** of the group, a few were **followers** and a couple were **sleepers** (very quiet).

The **sleepers** went in first, the **talker** had the job of motivating and the **followers** lacked the courage to do anything but were waiting for an opening.

Knife Attacks

Knife attacks account for the majority of serious physical crime. More and more people are using them, and the ease at which they can be concealed and acquired makes them a perfect weapon. One consolation with regards to knife attacks is that the person using the knife is usually someone who lacks the confidence to fight with their bear hands! Hence the need for a knife, but the way the knife is held will tell you a little

about the level of experience the person holding it has.

In this section we will look at the most common attack situations with a knife and I will explain some of the best defences, based on my own personal experiences and training in the military.

(If running is not an option)

Strike Points To The Face

When striking across the face with an Open Palm Heel Strike, consider the target areas. Here are a few targets for you to consider rather than just slapping an attacker across the face.

The nose will break if you follow through with the strike. If not the eyes will water and the attacker will be temporarily blinded allowing you to escape. (**Picture A**)

Picture A   **Picture B**   **Picture C**

The face will sting and knock the attacker over, This strike is useful if you intend to follow-up with another technique. (**Picture B**)

The ear if the hand is cupped (as in **Picture C**) will burst the ear drum, but considerable force and speed needs to be applied to this strike for it to work.

The face is a very sensitive area perhaps with the exception of the groin! Any strike here whether on target or not will deter most attackers. Please bear in mind the chapter *'Self Defence'* and especially what is 'reasonable force'. Needless to say the responsibility of the student is great. The more you learn the more responsibility you carry to be sensible.

In fact there is a strong case that could argue you should avoid conflict rather than face it head on. Water flows over and around an obstacle a lot easier than through it.

Knife Attacks
(Defending and Disarming)

Defender applies X Block

Pulls the arm down and around

Still holding the arm pull up to break the elbow joint

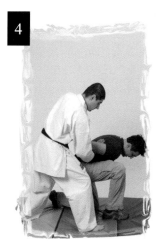

Continue to pull up and the attacker will drop to the floor

Knife Attacks
(Defending and Disarming)

Attacker lunges with a straight abdomen jab

Grab the arm and rotate with the elbow ready to strike

Striking to ribs but still holding the wrist with the knife

Left front kick to the groin

Knife Attacks
(Defending and Disarming)

**Grab the hand with
both arms**

**Pulling kick at the
same time**

**Grab the arm and start
to rotate**

**Hold the arm pull
up to break**

Knife Attacks
(Defending and Disarming)

The Face off or confrontation position

Attacker attempts a slash across the face with the knife.

Defender allows the slash then contacts the arm with the forearm

Pulling down at the same time attacking with the knee into the ribs.

Stress Management

Rather than teaching in this chapter forms of meditation which I am not qualified to do, I would like to point out activities that would increase your ability to stay calm and relax. We spend too much time worrying about the little things in our lives and not enough with the things that really should matter.

Stress is a condition that we feel is unmanageable because of the pressures of work or personal life that we can no longer control. The burdens of modern day living speak for themselves. Mortgages, loss of employment, family problems, violence at home, lack of understanding between partners, affairs, and many more real issues that affect our ability to control our lives or make sense of the world we live in.

Some Basic Considerations and Practical Ideas for relieving stress

Job satisfaction is important. Find a job that you would like to do, if you are not sure get advice. Work towards it, nice to have a goal or objective.

Yoga can be very fulfilling and also a good way of introducing meditation to beginners. Other forms of physical relaxation are **Pilates.**

Breathing and getting more oxygen into the brain is good way to relax. Usually in through the nose and out through the mouth deep breaths and for a minute or two.

Stress Management

Discuss problems Tell someone you trust – such as a teacher, parent or friend.

Silence find a place where you can have some peace and quiet and enjoy silence. No talking, no movement and no distractions. Doing nothing is sometimes better than something!

Healthy balanced diet can play a very important part in how you feel, put this together with excessive smoking and lack of sleep and you can soon understand the reasons for feeling fatigued. Plus consider the long term effects on the body that the above will have which can be damaging.

Manage Emotions these are both a cause of, and a result of conflict. People in conflict may have a variety negative emotions - anger, distrust, disappointment, frustration, confusion, worry, or fear. If you are having trouble staying calm, leave the room and come back to it later.

Resist correcting someone who has an incorrect understanding of something. We can do this by asking ourselves, ***"Does it really matter in the long run?"*** and **"Will it do more damage than good for me to show him or her that they are wrong?"**

Your not perfect. Develop a sense of well being where you are allowed to be wrong and make mistakes i.e. you are human after all.

Stress Management

Take control of your emotions does not always mean you get to win. Some advice on dealing with anger from **Brigham Young University's website** states there are a number of ways we can deal with anger, which include the following:

Go directly to the person we are angry with and try to settle our differences before getting other people involved.

Give in occasionally rather than always having to be right.

Keep a Perspective on things. Look at the bigger picture, this can help you feel motivated and in return challenge you to work harder and get more out of what you are doing. After living in Asia for a while I realised just how good things were back at home, and what I had taken for granted that so many people would give the right arm for. Why worry about a chore for next week, when you should be dealing with the present. Let next week take care of itself!

Forward Stance / **Zenkutsu Dachi**	**Prepare**	**Right Back Kick /** **Migi Ushiro Geri**

Eye Contact!

Self Defence

Law Library's Lexicon On Self-Defence

Each country has it's own interpretation and legal stance as to what is reasonable force. If you are unsure please contact your local Police Station who will be able to provide you with leaflets on current legislation in your country. What the definition below helps you understand is that self defence is a difficult arena to be in and the assailant instigating the attack can sometimes win if the defender does not use good judgement and control to evaluate what action, if any should be taken.

DEFENCE, SELF-DEFENCE - A defence to certain criminal charges involving force (e.g. murder). Use of force is justified when a person reasonably believes that it is necessary for the protection of oneself or another against the immediate use of unlawful force.

Pulling the head away is the normal reaction but wrong

Defender raises her arm inside attackers

Self Defence

Law Library's Lexicon On Self-Defence

However, a person must use no more force than appears reasonably necessary in the circumstances.

Force likely to cause death or great bodily harm is justified in self-defence only if a person reasonably believes that such force is necessary to prevent death or great bodily harm.

The Right To Protect One's Person And Property From Injury.

It will be proper to consider: **1.** The extent of the right of self-defence. **2.** By whom it may be exercised. **3.** Against whom. **4.** For what causes.

Puts those beautiful nails into action

Defender can now walk away from the assault

Self Defence

As to the extent of the right: First, when threatened violence exists, it is the duty of the person threatened to use all prudent and precautionary measures to prevent the attack; for example, if by closing a door which was usually left open, one could prevent an attack, it would be prudent, and perhaps the law might require, that it should be closed in order to preserve the peace.

Secondly, if after having taken such proper precautions, a party should be assailed, he may undoubtedly repel force by force, but in most instances cannot, under the pretext that he has been attacked, use force enough to kill the assailant or

Attackers Control and Threat Psychology

**Attacker grabs the
defenders neck**

**Then raises arm
as a threat**

Self Defence

hurt him after he has secured himself from danger; such as if a person unarmed enters a house to commit a burglary, while there he does not threaten any one, nor does any act which manifests an intention to hurt any one, and there are a number of persons present who may easily secure him, no one will be justifiable to do him any injury, much less to kill him; he ought to be secured and delivered to the public authorities. But when an attack is made by a thief under such circumstances, and it is impossible to ascertain to what extent he may push it, the law does not requite the party assailed to weigh with great nicety the probable extent of the attack, and he may use the most violent means against his assailant.

Attackers Control and Threat Psychology

Point your right index finger to the throat

Apply pressure carefully as necessary to get a release

Are Attacks Random or Premeditated?

We have already studied the various types of attackers in previous chapters. This explains why people attack and become violent.

For example we said that the *'Explosive attacker'* is looking for any excuse to attack - eye contact the most common in the infamous high street brawls!

Walk away, however hard this may be irrespective of the abuse. The verbal abuse is designed to get your reaction and nothing else – remember that! The conflict is verbally induced through and to a certain extent your involvement depends on whether you can swallow your pride and let it go.

Abuse always escalates and seldom de-escalates when both parties have been *'wound up'*. It takes a great deal of self-control to walk away! Karate teaches self control and hence increases your ability to walk away from conflict. Backing down from conflict does not make you a coward – it means your smart!

So what made you the recipient of the abuse? Your demeanour for one thing. If you look like you lack confidence you become an instant target. Training will improve your confidence. But just like car insurance no one wants to have it until something goes wrong then it becomes priceless. It's all too easy to drop out of training and make excuses.

Too busy, not enough time in the day but you owe yourself at least 1 hour a week to train and develop skills that may one day save your life.

Are Attacks Random or Premeditated?

Think about that, you are *'Life Preservation Training'*!

Take more caution in the things you do daily. A quick scan of an area and using your ears is a clear example. Around a parked car note visual obstacles– try and park in open areas never hidden away behind a large obstacle. Lock your car even for the shortest of moments. (paying your fuel bill at the petrol station) or at traffic lights.

Avoid getting into a routine most attackers observe their victims and 'note things!' **Premeditated attacks** are likely to occur once the assailant has worked out your routine it is then just about timing.

Under Attack At Borders Book Store

Are Attacks Random or Premeditated?

What is a routine?

- **When you go shopping**
- **When you arrive home from school, work or Karate?**
- **Are you married or not? Therefore do you live alone?**

Arriving home if you see something unusual, evaluate the situation beforehand. Drawn curtains, or lights on?

CALL THE POLICE FROM A NEIGHBOUR'S HOUSE OR MOBILE PHONE BUT DO NOT ENTER!

If you are at home and you suspect a break-in, lock yourself in the safest room possible and make sure you have access to a phone in that room. Consider your home and whether you have access to such a room. Install a good lock and it auto-matically becomes safer.

Visual Deterrents & Deceptions

Anything that promotes a positive impression for your well be-ing and safety is a deterrent. Wearing a wedding ring or en-gagement ring when you are not married can reduce your chances of being harassed by men.

Eye contact shows assertiveness rather than shying away from people. Keep your back straight, head up and arms to your side are positive signs together with the briskness that you use to walk.

Arms folded across the chest are very defensive stances and although natural in the way it feels gives a very protective and submissive message to an attacker.

Are Attacks Random or Premeditated?

Random Attacks

We never believe it will happen to us, so the brain is not prepared for it and hence the guard drops. This is when the **attacker attacks!** Not when you are ready but when you are unprepared, at your weakest and most relaxed state.

Random attacks are more likely to occur at night. How can we reduce the risk? Well one major step in the right direction is adapting for walking at night. Avoid poorly lit streets even if it is the shortest route home. Consider catching a taxi rather than saving money. Park in safe areas and understand that what appears safe at daytime looks completely unsafe to walk at night.

Always plan an escape route! Take a look around a parked area. It takes a few minutes to get adjusted for travel, seatbelts, lights, ignition—just the time an attacker needs!!

Take some premeditated safety measures! Try not to keep anything in your purse that has your address on it. If you have your drivers license stolen, it will give an attacker a lot of free information about you. (Single, age, address, etc. If you lose your keys remember after the shock of the ordeal - you have just turned a *random* attack into a *premeditated* one for later). Guaranteed the only thing you will be doing that day is cancelling cards lost not changing locks!

Are Attacks Random or Premeditated?

Keep your money in different pockets. If a mugger asks for your purse hand it over, they are not likely to check it in front of you, and you still have some cash to get home with!

The cycle in a violent attack is:

SHOCK
What is going on?

PAIN
Being hit and pushed around

ANGER
How could this happen to me?

Attacker moves in grabs right arm

Defender rotates her arm clockwise around the wrist

Are Attacks Random or Premeditated?

Here are some of the qualities that appeal to attackers and make you more of a target. Consider some of these factors as attackers are guided by what they see:

What you are wearing
How much jewellery is on show
Are you on your own
Any noticeable disabilities? Arm in sling?

> ***So therefore premeditated attacks are 'routine driven' and random attacks are 'image driven'***

Grabbing the attackers forearm

Left arm above the elbow apply down pressure

Are Attacks Random or Premeditated?
Self Risk Assessment

Spending a few moments to evaluate your own state of health is just as important as assessing the risk that a person poses to you. Making an informed decision on whether to drive or not if you have been drinking is reasonable and so should the following as well be.

If you are limping because of injury bear this in mind when walking home. **"Can you run to safety if you had to?"**

Here are a few examples of how to Self Risk Assess:

Sleep Deprivation — get plenty of it. This will keep you alert. Leaving the house half asleep reduces your chances of winning a conflict. Remember what I mentioned before:
> *'an attacker attacks when you're not ready'.*

Skirts and short dresses — I am not going dictate how you should dress, but consider what you are wearing? A short skirt may not allow you to kick or even run. If knocked down to the floor it may even restrict you.

**Forward Stance /
Zenkutsu Dachi**

**Preparation on both
attacker and defender part**

Are Attacks Random or Premeditated?

Stilettos — These can be a formidable weapon if used properly but running to safety is nearly impossible, if you have time - take them off and run. Most attackers will quit when faced with stubbornness.

Heavy bags — try not to keep anything expensive in the bag and drop it to speed up your escape - what is there in the bag that needs rescuing?

Jewellery on show — attracts attention and makes you a target. It looks nice but there is a right time to wear them.

Poor Health — When feeling unwell your senses are not operating at their best.

Choose your friends carefully — If they are violent, or aggressive, guess who they attract?

**Front Kick / Downward Block
Mae Geri / Gedan Barai**

**Reverse punch /
Gyaku Zuki**

Are Attacks Random or Premeditated?
Guidelines For Avoiding Injury & Attack

Attracting attention is a positive way of avoiding attack. Since no assailant wants the encounter to drag on.

(i) **Screaming and shouting** to attract attention and in most instances frighten the attacker.

(ii) **Dial 999** on your phone even if you cannot talk to the police because of the attacker, speaking out loud will alert the operator to what is going on and can be valuable evidence in the future.

(iii) **Mind your surroundings** — Get behind a physical barrier, table or car, anything that creates an obstacle between you and the attacker.

(iv) **Personal Alarms** — whistles, or personal attack sirens can very useful - some are deafening, while others deter!

(v) **Plan Exit** — never walk into anywhere or anyplace without planning a safe exit route should you need to use it.

(vii) **Lock Yourself Up** — even for the shortest of trips, in America most car crimes occur at night when the car is stationary at traffic lights. It has started here as well, namely London. Set off the car alarm, honk your horn anything that attracts attention dial 999.

(viii) **Nothing Is As It Seems** — If you see a suspicious person standing in front of your home or school report it to a teacher, they will not bite your head off and you may have saved a life!

Are Attacks Random or Premeditated?

Guidelines For Avoiding Injury & Attack

(ix) **Distraction Assaults** — If you are unsure about a person walk away. Does it really matter if you have got it wrong?

(x) **Increase Visibility** — make your presence known to people around you and so if you are staying behind to work late in an office, school or gym make sure there are people who know this. Namely security staff or your fellow colleagues.

(xi) **Why?** — if you know an area is not safe. Why do we feel the urge to investigate it?

(xii) **Money In The Bank** — Cash point Machines; take a good look before using one, and try to use the machines provided within a bank if possible where they are usually monitored by cameras. If this is not possible use one in an area well lit and in view of the general public.

(xiii) **Try to act more confident** – even if you don't feel it

(xiv) **Handle Verbal Abuse Better**– swearing no matter how bad, are just words, used to get a response. If it bothers you walk away from it, soon you will hear no more.

> *'Each successful encounter only increases confidence levels for the next one, the attacker is on a learning curve'*

Etiquette (Japanese protocol)

All karateka (karate practitioners) should bow on entering and leaving the Dōjō (training place).

●All karateka should bow to senior grades, irrespective of grade, within each association the seniority of grade is understood as all black belts look the same only the students will know.

●Immediately on entering the dojo line up in approximate positions ready for the lesson and start to loosen up by stretching rather than congregating in one corner of the Dōjō, or holding a conversation within a friend. Remember the Dōjō is for training and absorbing knowledge , it also shows the instructor you are ready to start.

Defender faces away as at a cash machine

Attacker grabs hair in effort to control & scare

Etiquette (Japanese protocol)

●When told to do so line up quickly in grade order, from front to back and right to left - the most senior grades line up to the left but this may vary from association to associa-tion.

●Lines should be straight with no gaps, i.e. you should always be in line with and directly behind someone. Lines should not be staggered unless told to do so.

●Late arrivals should make themselves known to the instruc-tor by kneeling at the side of the dojo until given permis-sion to join the class and then only by running behind all grades to take up their position as to not distract anyone.

Defender raises left arm right arm on top to augment the elbow strike

Defender strikes with the elbow to the abdomen

Etiquette (Japanese protocol)

●Stances should be maintained (for as long as reasonable) during any part of the session unless the command "Yame" (stop) is given.

●There should be no talking during the session and especially whilst the instructor is explaining something to other grades.

●When told to do so line up quickly in grade order, from front to back and right to left - the most senior grades line up to the left but this may vary from association to association.

●Karate discipline and etiquette is not only for the Dōjō but in public a shorter and more discreet bow would not be out of place when approaching a senior instructor or grade.

●Make sure your Gi (karate uniform) is clean

●Respect should be shown to all karateka from Dan grades to beginners.

> *'These rules should be strictly enforced by the instructor and senior grades, so as to maintain discipline and standards, something that today is becoming a lost art!'*

What Is Fatigue?

Fatigue as a concept is extremely hard to define, since everybody has their own idea of what being tired means. Everybody is tired once in a while - the most common reason is, of course, lack of sleep…

Fatigue can also be caused by a wide range of illnesses and diseases. In such cases, a person usually finds they suddenly (or even gradually) need more rest and sleep. This may affect their performance in everything. Fatigue is also common when you are feeling down.

Chronic Fatigue is a condition that causes exhaustion and fatigue without explanation. There is no hard and fast test for this syndrome, but it is diagnosed 'by exclusion'. This means that if doctors have tested for everything else without success, this is the only possibility left. Chronic fatigue is nonetheless a real condition. Although it is not directly treatable, it can be managed well enough to allow people to return to good health in time.

Acute Fatigue Acute fatigue results from short-term sleep loss or from short periods of heavy physical or mental work. The effects of acute fatigue are of short duration and usually can be reversed by sleep and relaxation.

Signs and Symptoms of fatigue include:

- tiredness,
- sleepiness, including falling asleep against your will ("micro" sleeps),
- irritability,
- depression,
- giddiness,
- loss of appetite,
- digestive problems, and
- increased susceptibility to illness

If you suffer from fatigue whatever the type, you become irritable, irritation leads to aggression, guess what that leads to?

Body Language & The Wolf

In psychology and other social and behavioural sciences "aggression" refers to behaviour that is intended to cause harm or pain. Aggression can be either physical or verbal and behaviour is classified as 'aggression' even if it does not actually succeed in causing harm or pain. Property damage and other destructive behaviour may also fall under the definition of aggression.

Behaviours like aggression can be learned by watching and imitating the behaviour of others. A considerable amount of evidence suggests that watching violence on television increases the likelihood of violent behaviour in children and adults. Individuals may differ in how they respond to violence. The greatest impact is on those who are already prone to violent behaviour.

Aggression is a perplexing phenomenon. Why are people motivated to hurt each other? How does violence help organisms to survive and reproduce? After two centuries of theories psychologists and other scientists have been able to look deeply into aggression's biological and evolutionary roots, as well as its consequences.

An animal defending itself against a predator becomes aggressive in order to survive and to ensure the survival of its offspring. Because aggression against a much larger enemy or group of enemies would lead to the death of an animal, animals have developed a good sense of when they are outnumbered or outgunned. This ability to gauge the strength of other animals gives animals a **"fight or flight"**
response to predators; depending on how strong they gauge the predator to be animals will either become aggressive or flee.

Body Language & The Wolf

According to many researchers, predatory behaviour is not aggression. Cats do not hiss or arch their backs when in pursuit of a mouse.

Aggression against co-species serves a number of purposes having to do with breeding. One of the most common purposes is the establishment of a dominance hierarchy. When certain types of animals are first
placed in a common environment, the first thing they do is fight to assert their role in the dominance hierarchy. Fighting amongst themselves would not be beneficial for a given species because of the
injuries it would cause. In establishing itself in a dominance hierarchy, an animal also sets its attractiveness. In a variety of species, a high social ranking means more and healthier mates. Thus, while aggression carries the risk of wounding the animal, it benefits the animal by giving its offspring healthier genes if it is successful in the hierarchy.

There are a number of comparisons that can be monitored when analysing aggression, in the human and animal context.

The question that needs to be asked, has our modern society resulted, in the breakdown of our basic application of aggression? Once a female has given birth to an offspring, this female develops maternal aggression. This maternal aggression is directed mainly at co-species and is believed intended to prevent the mother's offspring from harassment by individuals.

In our daily lives we encounter many forms of body language gestures, these are a few examples:

"Stress": Shaking of legs

Body Language & The Wolf

"Lying": Face turned away, no eye contact, or looking to the left (fabricating information). Also wiping hands on trousers to get rid of sweat or fidgeting with hands

"Aggression": Clenched fists, squaring of shoulders, stiffening of posture, tensing of muscles

"Anxiety": Massaging temples, different than normal breathing rates, hunched shoulders, nervous head movements

Animal Body Language in "Wolves" can visually communicate an impressive variety of expressions and moods that we can relate to humans.

"Dominance": A dominant wolf stands stiff legged and tall. The ears are erect and forward, and the shackles bristle slightly. Often the tail is held vertical and curled toward the back. This display shows the wolf's rank to all others in the pack. A dominant wolf may stare at a submissive pack member, pin it to the ground, "ride up" on its shoulders, or even stand on its hind legs.

Forward Stance / Ready
Zenkutsu Dachi / Yoi

Straight Punch / X Block
Oi Zuki / Juji Uke

Body Language & The Wolf

"Anger" An angry wolf's ears are erect, and its fur bristles. The lips may curl up or pull back, and the incisors are displayed. The wolf may also arch its back, lash out, or snarl.

"Fear" A frightened wolf tries to make its body look small and therefore less conspicuous. The ears flatten down against the head, and the tail may be tucked between the legs, as with a submissive wolf. There may also be whimpering or barks of fear, and it may arch its back.

"Defensive" A defensive wolf flattens its ears against its head.

"Aggression" An aggressive wolf snarls and its fur bristles. The wolf may crouch, ready to attack if necessary.

"Suspicion" Pulling back of the ears shows a wolf is suspicious. In addition, the wolf narrows its eyes. The tail of a wolf that senses danger points straight out, parallel to the ground.

"Relaxedness" A relaxed wolf's tail points straight down, and the wolf may rest sphinx-like or on its side. The wolf may also wag its tail. The further down the tail droops, the more relaxed the wolf is.

Defender pulls right arm back to hip

Reverse Punch / Gyaku Zuki

Body Language & The Wolf

Therefore by observing animals we learn a great deal about our own evolutionary development as it pertains to aggression and body language. Namely what impression we portray to an attacker, and how confident we feel. All of these things without speaking!

Karate For Children

Benefits of Training?

Growing up used to be less traumatic a decade ago. A 1993 poll found more than half the children questioned said they were afraid of violent crime against them or a family member. Are they just paranoid, or is there a real problem? Girls seem to be at greater risk. They are all too aware of the dangers and seem to mature quicker than most boys with regards to training. In my classes the boys just want to learn to fight whereas the girls want to learn self defence! I find in Lower schools they are shielded, but as soon as they start middle school the goal posts change considerably. Their bodies are developing and boys take more of an interest in them. They are given the freedom to walk home on their own, or catch the bus and all these are factors and make the case for teaching karate vitally credible.

It doesn't stop there. The higher they climb the education ladder the harder it becomes from a safety point of view. College courses run later in the evening and University degrees moves them away from their parents and family homes, for a sustained period of time.

Bringing up children is hard enough without having to worry about their safety away from home. Karate does not take away the fears but it does reduce it. Knowing that your child is being careful and vigilant will give a little extra peace of mind. Consequently we start teaching from the age 5 and above. This may seem young but good habit formation and training will set them up for the future. If they leave which some do what they have learnt they take with them so we win either way really.

Karate For Children

Awareness

We cannot replace or get rid of the dangers in our society but with regular training Karate can help the student understand and avoid situations which may potentially become volatile.

Drive and Determination

A responsible instructor should prepare students for life. Through quarterly exams, the students develop their own drive and desire to succeed by applying techniques learned and demonstrating them to a panel of examiners. This is key and believe or not girls in general do better than the boys. This section highlights the responsibility of parents to invest in the safety of their children through a reputable Karate school or any other established and properly running club.

Choosing an Instructor

- Make sure the Instructor is Enhanced CRB Checked to work with children—they should be happy to show it to you. (check their certificate is not over 2 years old)

- Has the necessary qualifications to teach young adults i.e. coaching certificate, level of experience.

- Attend a class first before you sign up to assess suitability

- Ask to see their qualifications of rank attained they should be able to show their full history

- Instructors Public / Professional Indemnity Insurance which will highlight that an organisation has approved them for insurance. i.e. they have met a criteria for insurance purposes.

- Charging of classes varies from Instructor to Instructor, but an After School Club should resemble the fees paid for any other activity at the school. (I mention this as there is some heavy over charging).

- Examinations are normally held every 3 months and are 'not compulsory' but nice for the student to progress to a new grade.

- Parents can watch examinations but as the student progresses in grade the exam waiting time and indeed actual examination extend in duration and hence leaving students to perform exams becomes common practice.

- Schools that hire a hall to an instructor should see legal documents highlighting the above, In all of the schools I teach that was the first thing they asked to see, a sign of a good school.

The Aggressive Handshake and Release

Some handshakes can escalate and after asking to be released if this fails here is an option.

Normal handshake

Grab the wrist with the free hand (left).

Rotate the right hand up to grab the thumb

Push back on the thumb to force attacker to sit down.

Japanese Terminology

A

Age:Lift up (Rising technique)
Age-Uke: (Jodan-uke): Upper block
Age-zuki: Upward punch
Ate-waza: Hitting techniques

B

C

Choku: Straight
Chudan: Middle
Chudan-choku-zuki: Middle straight punch
Chudan-shuto-uke: Middle knife-hand block

D

Dachi: Stance
Dojo: Gym, training hall. Literally 'Way Place'

E

Empi: Elbow
Empi uchi: Elbow strike

F

Fudo-dachi: Inverted parallel stance
Fumikomi: Downward (stomping) kick

G

Gedan: Low
Gedan-kekomi: Low thrust kick
Gedan-zuki: Low punch
Gedan-Uke: Low block
Gi: Karate Uniform
Gyaku-zuki: Reverse punch

Japanese Terminology

H
Hachiji-dachi: Natural stance (hip width 45 foot angle)
Haishu: Back hand (open hand)
Haishu uchi: Back hand strike
Haishu uke: Back hand block
Haisoku: Upper part of foot
Haito: Ridge hand
Haito uchi: Ridgehand strike
Hajime: Begin or start (command given ofr sparring competition)
Hangetsu-dachi: Half-moon Stance
Hanmi: Forward Stance with hip at 45
Heiko-dachi: Parallel stance
Heisoku-dachi: Informal attention stance
Hidari: Left
Hiji: Elbow
Hiji-ate: Elbow strike
Hiji-uchi: Elbow strike
Hiraken: Hand technique where the fingers are bent at the first finger joint
Hittsui: Knee
Hizagashira: Knee cap

I

J
Ju-Kumite: Free Sparring
Jodan: Upper
Jodan-age-uke: Upper/upward block
Jodan-choku-zuki: High straight punch
Jodan-kekomi: High thrust kick
Jodan-mae-geri: High front kick
Juji-uke: Cross hand blockand

Japanese Terminology

K
Kagi-zuki: Hook punch
Kaisho: Open hand
Kakuto: Heel
Karate: Empty Hand
Kata: Form (Sequence or movement)
Keage: Snap Kick
Kekomi: Thrust Kick
Kentsui: Outside edge of the hand when clenched
Keri (Geri): Kick
Keri-waza: Kicking technique
Kiba-dachi: Horse stance
Kihon-Kumite: Basic Sparring
Kizami-zuki: Jab
Kokutsu-dachi: Back stance (70 weight on the back leg, 30 on the front)
Ko-Shi: Ball of the foot
Kumite: Sparring

L
M
Mae-ashi-geri: Kick with the front leg
Mae-empi-uchi: Front elbow strike
Mae-geri: Front kick
Mae-geri-keage: Front snap kick
Mae-hiji-ate: Forward elbow strike
Makiwara: A board rooted in the ground used to hit to practice focus
Mawashi-geri: Roundhouse kick
Mawashi-zuki: Roundhouse punch
Migi: Right
Mikazuki-geri: Crescent kick (Kick with the inside of the foot)
Modotte: Command to return to original spot or posture.

Japanese Terminology

N
Nai-wan: Nami-ashi-geri: Crecent kick (block) Neko-ashi-dachi: Nukite: knife hand strike (palm flat, strike with finger tips)

O
O-Sensei: Founding sensei of the style (Tsuyoshi Chitose for Chito Ryu Karate)
O-Uchi Mawashi geri: Roundhoouse kick (From back leg)

P Q

R
Rei: Bow Ren zuki: Continuous punches Rohai: Kata Name Ryote: Double (strike or block) Ryu San: Kata Name Rinten: Full turn (techniques involving a turn of 360°)

S
Seiza: Sit (command)
San Shin: Kata Name
Shi Ho Hai: Kata Name
San Shi Riu: Kata Name
Seisan: Kata Name
Soto (uke): Outside (block)
Sukui Uke: Scooping block
Sayuzuki: Double strike (usually in shiko dachi)

T
Tai sabaki: body movement (evasive techniques)
Tettsui uchi: Strike with bottom of closed fist (aka kensui uchi)
Tenshin: Kata Name
Te-Hodoki: Hand release techniques
Te: Hand (kara-TE = empty hand)
Tsuki: punch (aka Zuki)
Tanden: Lower abdomen, seat of Ki or Chi
Temeshiwara: Breaking techniques

Japanese Terminology

U
Uke: Block
Ura: Upside down or inverted

V W X

Y
Yoko: Side Yame: Stop (command)
Yoi: Begin (command)
Yama Zuki: Y-Block (one hand down, one hand over head)

Z
Zuki: punch (aka Tsuki)

Resources

Guidance on the 'use of reasonable' force by householders to defend themselves, their families and homes can be obtained from the Crown Prosecution Service website:

http://www.cps.gov.uk/publications/prosecution/ householders.html

Or from CPS Communications Branch Tel: 0207 7796 8442
Or email: **publicity.branch@cps.gsi.gov.uk**

More Advice on Preventing Crime

Your local police station will be able to give you helpful advice on preventing crime. Some check your home or business premises and recommend ways to improving the security.
This is a popular service, and if there is a waiting list a information tion pack will be sent out t allow you to check yourself. You can get useful advice from:- **www.crimeprevention.gov.uk** or the police website follow the links **www.securedbydesign.com.**

ChildLine is the free helpline for children and young people in the UK. Children and young people can call us on **0800 1111** to talk about any problem – our counsellors are always here to help you sort it out

On **www.donthideit.com,** you can hear about other children's experiences and find help and advice about tackling abuse.
You can also create a badge to show your support for ending child abuse.

Karate Grades

The grades awarded vary from association to association but here is a definitive guide as to the most commonly used system. Grades before Black belt are **KYU Grades** and above **Dan Grades**.

ORDER OF GRADES

White Belt	-	'Ungraded'
Blue Belt	-	'10th Kyu'
Red Belt	-	'9th kyu'
Orange	-	'8th Kyu'
Orange / Yellow Stripe	-	'8th Kyu' Inter
Yellow	-	'7th kyu'
Yellow / Green Stripe	-	'7th Kyu' Inter
Green Belt	-	'6th Kyu'
Green / Purple Stripe	-	'6th Kyu' Inter
Purple Belt	-	'5th Kyu'
Purple / 2 White Stripes	-	'4th Kyu'
Brown Belt	-	'3rd Kyu'
Brown / White Stripe	-	'2nd Kyu'
Brown / Red Stripe	-	'1st Kyu'
Black Belt	-	'1st Dan'

There are 10 KYU grades and 10 Dan Grades. (the intermediate grades are not counted as they only help prepare the student for a smaller jump to the full grade as a result of the learning and to avoid knocking confidence levels) The normal requirement for regular training is that a student depending on their ability and number of sessions completed, grade every 3 months for a new grade. The certification for that grade allows the student to wear the new belt and in the months that follow prove worthy of the grade awarded. Seniority is based on rank first and not age, Thus, all are equal but their skill and time in training set them apart from each other.

References

President Hashemi Rafsanjani (IR Of Iran)
Liberal Democrat Party Survey on Violence in London
Lectric Law Library's Lexicon On Self Defence
The Alliance of the Guardian Angels History website
UK Guardian Angels Office, Simon Burley
Wikipedia, the free encyclopaedia
Physical Violence in American Families, 1990
Crime in England and Wales 04/05 Home Office Report
Mind Tools Ltd on Stress management definition
Conflict Research Consortium, University of Colorado, USA
Sensei Funakoshi, (The 20 Precepts)
Home Office Statistical Bulletin 6/01, May 2001
Personal reference by Jane North
Joachim Gruppe 5th Dan JKA Berlin, Germany
Home Office Communication Directorate.2005 Ref:268853.
Laura Hutchinson Biggleswade Chronicle
Simon Hutchinson Beds On Sunday
Ross Andrew Thomson

For all your Martial Arts Supplies the Author Recommends:-

Playwell Martial Arts
Playwell House
30-31 Sheraton Business Centre
Wadsworth Road
Perivale
Middlesex
UB6 7JB
www.playwell.co.uk

Meijin
141Goldhawks Road
Shepherds Bush
London
W12 8EN
0208 749 9070
www.meijin.co.uk

The Grandmaster's 20 Precepts

1. Karate-do begins with courtesy and ends with rei.
2. There is no first strike in karate.
3. Karate is an aid to justice.
4. First know yourself before attempting to know others.
5. Spirit first, technique second.
6. Always be ready to release your mind.
7. Accidents arise from negligence.
8. Do not think that karate training is only in the dojo.
9. It will take your entire life to learn karate, there is no limit.
10. Put your everyday living into karate and you will find "Myo" (subtle secrets).
11. Karate is like boiling water, if you do not heat it constantly, it will cool.
12. Do not think that you have to win, think rather that you do not have to lose.
13. Victory depends on your ability to distinguish vulnerable points from invulnerable ones.
14. The out come of the battle depends on how you handle weakness and strength.
15. Think of your opponents hands and feet as swords.
16. When you leave home, think that you have numerous opponents waiting for you.
17. Beginners must master low stance and posture, natural body positions are for the advanced.
18. Practicing a kata exactly is one thing, engaging in a real fight is another.
19. Do not forget to correctly apply: strength and weakness of power, stretching and contraction of the body, and slowness and speed of techniques.
20. Always think and devise ways to live the precepts of karate-do every day.

by Master Gichin Funakoshi
(1868-1957)

My dear friend Paul, thank you for introducing me to Karate, it has been a part of my life for a quarter of a century.

May you rest in peace old friend!